Andrew Klavan has written a stunningly original work that defies classification by genre. It is, at once, literary, philosophical, and deeply Christian—and, for all those reasons, personally enriching. Klavan tells how the English Romantic poets—Coleridge, Wordsworth, Keats, and others—set about to use the artistic imagination to salvage "man's instinctive knowledge of the supernatural" just as materialistic philosophy was taking root in European intellectual circles during the early nineteenth century.

Klavan, a master storyteller, provides a fascinating and informative short history of these literary giants. In the process, he explains why their poetry is important and how it helped to reveal that "this seemingly indifferent universe is, in fact, a personal creator's act of love." Then, in a theological finale, he applies the insights of the great poets to illuminate the true meaning of some of the most challenging aspects of the teachings of Christ.

The Truth and Beauty is full of insight about romantic love and human mortality, the perils of utopian politics, the nature of men and women, the meaning of life and the moral order, science and the possibility of knowledge, and especially, the teachings of Jesus as recorded in the Gospels. Not since reading C. S. Lewis's *The Great Divorce* in college has a single book induced such deep and constructive theological reflection in me, as I suspect it will for many other readers.

—STEPHEN C. MEYER, PhD, author, *Return of the God Hypothesis: Three Scientific Discoveries That Reveal the Mind behind the Universe*; director, Center for Science and Culture, Discovery Institute, Seattle

What have the Romantic poets to do with Jerusalem? Quite a lot, it turns out. Andrew Klavan has long since secured his spot as one of the most brilliant writers of our age. In *The Truth and Beauty*, Klavan's cultural insight and eloquence shine as never before. The Romantics lived, as we do, in a time of disenchantment and unbelief. Through a deeply personal telling of his relationship with long-dead poets and the God who made both us and them, Klavan gently guides his readers away from the illusions of our age back toward the transcendentals.

—MICHAEL KNOWLES, author, no. 1 national bestselling *Speechless*; host, *The Michael Knowles Show*

We live in a disenchanted world, a world of commodities and "stuff" that simply do not satisfy the intrinsic human craving for meaning and transcendence. Even the church can too often be driven by prosaic consumerism and not by the great mysteries of life. This is, strange to tell, where some of the great giants of English literature, especially the Romantics, can help us. They may not have offered the right answers, but they did grasp something of the mystery of existence. In this book, Andrew Klavan uses these great writers as foils for discussing the deeper questions of life, questions which he shows are answered only in Christ. For those who love both Christ and great literature, as Andrew Klavan clearly does, this book is a delight and a means to that most important of things: the reenchantment of our world.

—CARL R. TRUEMAN, professor, biblical and religious studies, Grove City College; fellow, Ethics and Public Policy Center, D.C.

Poetry and literature point to the sacred. Andrew Klavan reminds us how.

—DR. JORDAN B. PETERSON, author, international bestselling *Maps of Meaning*, *Twelve Rules for Life*, and *Beyond Order*

You don't have to be a Christian to appreciate much of the timeless wisdom Andrew Klavan presents in *The Truth and Beauty*. Klavan is a magnificent writer, a person of wisdom, and a man of compassion—all of which shine through here.

—BEN SHAPIRO, editor emeritus, *Daily Wire*; host, *The Ben Shapiro Show*

THE TRUTH AND BEAUTY

THE TRUTH
AND BEAUTY

*How the Lives and Works of England's
Greatest Poets Point the Way to a Deeper
Understanding of the Words of Jesus*

ANDREW KLAVAN

ZONDERVAN
BOOKS

ZONDERVAN BOOKS

The Truth and Beauty
Copyright © 2022 by Amalgamated Metaphor, Inc.

Requests for information should be addressed to:
Zondervan, 3900 Sparks Dr. SE, Grand Rapids, Michigan 49546

Zondervan titles may be purchased in bulk for educational, business, fundraising, or sales promotional use. For information, please email SpecialMarkets@Zondervan.com.

ISBN 978-0-310-36463-4 (audio)

Library of Congress Cataloging-in-Publication Data

Names: Klavan, Andrew, author.
Title: The truth and beauty : how the lives and works of England's greatest poets point the way to a deeper understanding of the words of Jesus / Andrew Klavan.
Description: Grand Rapids : Zondervan, 2022. | Includes bibliographical references. | Summary: "The words of Jesus can be as mysterious as they are familiar. For those seeking greater understanding of the Gospels through storytelling and poetry comes this book by Andrew Klavan, who chronicles his own inspiring, late-in-life journey to achieve a fresh perspective and deep connection to Jesus's most well-known and complex biblical passages"—Provided by publisher.
Identifiers: LCCN 2021054616 (print) | LCCN 2021054617 (ebook) | ISBN 9780310364610 (hardcover) | ISBN 9780310364627 (ebook)
Subjects: LCSH: English literature—19th century—History and criticism. | Christianity and literature—Great Britain—History—19th century. | Bible and literature. | Jesus Christ—Teachings. | Romanticism—Great Britain.
Classification: LCC PR468.R44 K53 2022 (print) | LCC PR468.R44 (ebook) | DDC 820.9/382—dcundefined
LC record available at https://lccn.loc.gov/2021054616
LC ebook record available at https://lccn.loc.gov/2021054617

Cover design: Richard Ljoenes Design LLC
Cover photo: Menna / Reinhold Leitner / Shutterstock
Author photo: Kristyn Kimball Photography
Interior design: Sara Colley

Printed in the United States of America

22 23 24 25 26 27 28 29 30   /LSC/   12 11 10 9 8 7 6 5 4

For Nathan Edward Moore,
   a loving welcome

CONTENTS

ACKNOWLEDGMENTS

When I was planning this book, it was my dream to revisit some of the locations in which the events I describe take place. I imagined myself traveling back to the homes of Wordsworth and Coleridge in the English Lake District and to the Keats-Shelley museum that now occupies the Roman rooms where John Keats died. Perhaps I would see some of the original writings of these poets in their own hands, and speak with the curators who watch over them. But when the pandemic of 2020 struck and the world shut down, all my travel and speaking engagements were canceled, and I decided it would be wise to seize the tragic moment to do the work that had been haunting me for years. As a result, what I hoped to have accomplished on location and in the company of scholars was done in a workshop the size of an outhouse with a computer and a collection of my own decaying books strewn about the desk and floor. And while I always tried to use those tools to track down the original sources I cited, I was also always dependent upon and indebted to the scholarship of specialists who directed me to those sources. I could not have written this book if there were no M. H. Abrams or Jacques Barzun, Richard Holmes or Stephen Greenblatt, Walter Jackson Bate or Juliet Barker or all the other biographers, critics, and historians whom I tried to credit in the bibliography. It was very important to me to acknowledge their work, but at the same time, I was concerned not to involve them in my own sometimes unpopular points of view. I therefore cited them only in notes when a quotation or insight came from them specifically. If at any point I failed to mention someone deserving of credit, let me say simply that all the facts reported here were originally gathered by better scholars than myself. Only the interpretations of those facts are mine.

I am extremely grateful to my editor, Webster Younce, for his work on the book and even more grateful for his support as well as the support of HarperCollins Christian Publishing. I am also very thankful for the work of Don Fehr and all the agents at Trident Media Group. Ryley Constable did a wonderful job with the notes and bibliography, completing the work begun by Abigail Liebing.

A word of thanks also to Jeremy Boreing, Ben Shapiro, and all my friends at the *Daily Wire*, where I have been given a platform from which to speak my mind freely in a world where such platforms are increasingly rare. Creating *The Andrew Klavan Show* podcast has allowed me to refine my thoughts and field criticism on some of the ideas that inform this book, and also to reach a new audience eager to engage with Western culture in a fresh and meaningful way.

It's not enough to thank my son Spencer for giving me a helpful read of the manuscript—though he did and I'm grateful. But more than that, during our hikes up hills and into canyons, and in our late night discussions over whiskey and cigars, our ideas have interwoven and morphed and melded until it has become impossible for either of us to remember who said what first or how any given notion was shaped into its final form. In any case, I could not have written this book without knowing him.

That and more is also true of my wife, Ellen Treacy, who has elevated love to an art form, and elevated my art through her love. To her alone falls the unenviable task of reading my shambolic first drafts, into which I seem to throw every thought I ever had since childhood. When she heroically took on my earliest effort at *The Truth and Beauty*, she told me it was such a mess that there were times while reading it when she actually doubted my sanity. My serene reply should be printed on T-shirts and sold at writers conferences: "No, no, it's a great book. I just have to cut out all the bad parts." With her help and Webster's, I hope I have.

INTRODUCTION

Christ and the Romantics

1.

"I don't understand the Sermon on the Mount," I said.

It was just past midnight, New Year's Eve. I was sitting on a balcony with my son Spencer. We were eighteen floors up, as I remember. We were nursing whiskeys. Before us and below us stretched the lowlands of Miami, a city I have never loved. It's all abandoned canyons of white stone, vast boulevards empty of pedestrians as in a plague. The alien palms look like piniored spiders. The spiders are the size of alien palms. Sudden iguanas, giant lizards with their giant lizard eyes, stare at you from unexpected urban niches. People find alligators on their lawns and in their swimming pools. I don't like alligators.

One morning, I saw a corpse floating in the bay. As I stood in a crowd of onlookers, watching the policemen pull the dead man into their boat, the lady standing next to me said, "Yes. That happened to me a few weeks ago. I was swimming at the beach and one floated by." Bodies in the water are just a thing that happens here, in other words. In other words, the whole town stinks of crime and casual corruption.

Gaudy emptiness, monsters, and misconduct: it's a city modeled on the human heart, a microcosm of the bright and shiny world.

On top of which, the good news of winter never seems to reach the place. Here it was January, the first minutes of morning, and it was only now that the muggy heat of the long day had lifted. We sat on the balcony, my son and I, and watched the year ending. Fireworks bloomed across the darkling plain of the city, first here, then there, then near, then in the distance. I felt the pleasant melancholy of far-off celebrations.

My wife, my son, and I had come here for the holidays. We were visiting my daughter Faith, her husband, and their new-made son. During daylight hours, we would dawdle in the young family's apartment or go out to visit some tourist site or other when we could tolerate the heat. After the baby's bedtime, we visitors would retire to our rented high-rise apartment to let the parents rest. Finally, after my wife went to bed, Spencer and I would pour ourselves drinks, sit out on the balcony, and discuss religion, philosophy, and literature, the things we loved.

"I understand the words of the Sermon, obviously," I went on. "But I can never see the sense of it clearly. And even when I do, I'm not sure I believe in any of it or agree with it. The Beatitudes read to me like: 'Blessed are you when your life is awful, because in heaven, trust me, it's gonna be great.' I feel life is more essential than that. It's not a trivial throwaway. It's not a sentence you suffer in the flesh until you get to the good part when you're dead. Or what about, 'Don't resist an evil person?' Or, 'Love your enemy'? Or, 'Turn the other cheek'? I mean, we're so used to believing these are high moral commandments. They're the foundation stones of Western civilization, in a way. But would you actually do any of them in real life? Should you do them? Turn the other cheek? If an evil person attacked you, would I stand by with some prissy smile on my face, loving him and not resisting him? Congratulating myself on my piety? I'd rip his head off. I'd do my best to. If he attacked Mom, I'd kill him, then bring him back to life and kill him again just for the pleasure of it. And that would be the right thing to do, wouldn't it? Not stand there like some simpering parson. Does pretending to believe something is good when you can't live by it realistically— does that even mean anything? 'If you lust after someone, you've already committed adultery.' Well, no, you actually haven't. All right, I can come up with a way to think about that so that it has some truth to it. But it's not really true—not true like truth is true. So what's the point of it all?"

My son was studying for his doctorate in Classics at Oxford then. He knew more about almost everything than I did—except life, I guess, my being over sixty. He was a true scholar, like his mother's father before him, while I . . . I may fairly say that I had read just about everything there was to read in the world, every-thing worth reading anyway. I was a dogged completist in such matters. But I could never remember a word of anything I read. Images, descriptions of events, ideas—they all just seemed to pour themselves into some hobo bisque bubbling away in my brainpan until the steam of it rose behind my eyes as a visionary atmosphere, a general way of understanding things and seeing them. I was a novelist, in other words, an artist, a barefoot teller of tales, as I liked to say. When I looked out on the exterior landscape, I saw mostly what I imagined to be there. Like a blind man then, I found reality by the touch of it. I felt my way.

By this method, about a dozen years before, at nearly fifty, I had become a Christian. It was a bold decision, in one sense, a stroke against the unbelieving tenor of the times. But it was tentative too. I told myself I could always revert to being a secular Jew if Christ turned me superstitious or small minded or otherwise screwy. In the event, however, to my wonder and delight, it was all the other way around. Baptized, I had acquired a new realism. My deepened relationship with God augmented my talent for living. I would never call myself an easy creature, even now. I have always been an oversized and thumpy character who made the knickknacks rattle when I walked around. But accepting Christ had transformed me into a weirdly peaceful monster, joyful in every little thing. Not happy in everything—that would have just made me a loon. But alive to the life of the moment, and twice alive to the people and the things I loved: my family and my friends, my work and a good whiskey, a good book and the loveliness of enchanted venues, almost everywhere, in fact, that was not literally Miami.

Also, I had noticed this: each time I reached a deeper understanding of some passage in the gospel, each time I learned to adapt my mind just a little more to the mind of Christ, it was like swallowing a spoonful of crazy happy sauce. It made my joy increase, and I don't mean in the moment only but ever after, all the time.

So to founder on the Sermon on the Mount was a real frustration to me. It was like I had a great big jar of crazy happy sauce right in front of me and couldn't get the lid off. I wasn't going to explain away what made no sense to me—I hate that. I wouldn't quote back to myself some tidy piety from some book or sermon—I hate that too. And you know what else I hate? Windy nothingness: grandiose oratory that purports to elucidate gospel wisdom and then blows on out of your mind, leaving life just the same as always.

No. I believed in the Gospels now. I truly did. But I wanted to know what I believed, what exactly. If Jesus was the Word made flesh, let him speak to me. If he was God made man, let him speak to me man to man.

I said to my son, "The thing is, I have this intense feeling that it all does actually make sense somehow. It's like a beautiful picture, but it's blurry to me. I feel if I could just turn the lens a little bit this way or that, it would all come suddenly into focus. But I can't seem to do it."

Whereupon Spencer sipped his whiskey, watched the panorama of fireworks below, thought about it for a while, and said, "Maybe the problem is that you are trying to understand a philosophy instead of trying to get to know a man."

I recognized this on the instant as the single smartest thing anyone had ever said to me.

2.

To know someone, to really know him, is to see what he sees, at least a little. You can't do it just by understanding his philosophy. You have to get close to him. Walk with him. Hear his unsaid words, catch his inflections, do his bidding sometimes when it runs counter to your profit or your will. Do all that and, after a while, you find you've made some of his gestures or some turns of phrase or even some points of view a part of your own experiential repertoire. You can pick his voice out of a dozen voices, imagine what he would think or say if he were with you. You carry him in yourself like a second conscience, a counterpoint to your own silent soliloquy. To know someone is to become him in a small way and to let him become a part of you. The way we know our parents. The way we grow to know our spouses. The way we sometimes know those friends whom we love.

So I set out to get to know Jesus—at least a little. I used every tool I could think of to try to draw near.

I taught myself koine Greek—badly. I began to read the Gospels—haltingly—in their original tongue, or at least the oldest tongue we have them in. I worked myself up to five Greek lines a day, translating them into English with the help of all the miraculous modern gizmos I could assemble, and with the occasional less modern but equally miraculous help of my son, who reads ancient Greek like an ancient. I tried my best to look at Jesus as I would at any man on first meeting him, or as I would a character in a novel or a history first-time read. To this end, I forced myself to abandon every preexisting notion I had of him. I ignored every doctrine of theology, including those of the apostle Paul. I wanted Jesus direct, unfiltered by tradition. I wanted his words, his ideas, his vision, not what the saints and sermons said he said.

More than anything, I wanted to know him so I could understand what it was he was telling me to do day by day. I'm a simple man in this respect, a practical man. I'm less interested in plumbing the cosmos than I am in getting from here to sundown. I believe with all my heart that God is three persons, Father, Son, and Holy Ghost, but if it turns out he's five guys named Moe, I'm not going to cancel my vacation. I'm not a theologian. I'm not a pastor. You mustn't trust your salvation to me. It'll just get you into trouble.

But—fiercely, constantly—I want to know how to become the man God made me to be, how to do the works he created me to do. I trust him with the big questions of eternity. I trust him with the end of days. I trust him with the last judgment. He hasn't asked me for my opinion about them, so aside from the pure intellectual pleasure of imagining my enemies in hell, I see no reason to waste precious seconds trying to form one.

But he must have made me with a purpose. No? He must have given me this moment on the planet with a thought in mind. I want to know what it looks like to live that out to the fullest. Not just in some general sense. I didn't need God to die on a cross to tell me to be nice or charitable or faithful to my wife. I'm nice enough. I'm even charitable now and then. And I'm nuts about my wife; I'm always faithful. But I want to know second by second how the Logos instructed me to understand myself so I can have "joy to the full" and "life more abundantly" just as he promised.

On this question—what Jesus meant for us to do exactly—I think it's fair to say opinions differ. In the Nicene Creed, the most widely accepted statement of Christian orthodoxy, Jesus' ministry and preaching do not appear at all. His whole life hangs invisible in the empty space between two sentences.

> By the power of the Holy Spirit he became incarnate
> > from the Virgin Mary,
> and was made man.
> For our sake he was crucified under Pontius Pilate,
> he suffered death and was buried . . .[1]

That's it. He was born miraculously, and, suffering, he died. That's the savior's credal biography, start to finish. It's like being in one of those painting galleries in the museum's medieval wing:

picture after picture of the Madonna and Child, and picture after
picture of the crucifixion, but precious few pictures of what happened in between. A friend of mine once described it as getting the
bread of the sandwich without the meat in the middle.

This is not an oversight either. It's ancient dogma. It expresses
the idea that Christianity is an event, not a code of behavior.

"The gospel is good news, not good advice," popular preacher
Timothy Keller writes. "The gospel is not primarily a way of life.
It is not something we do, but something that has been done for us
and something that we must respond to."[2]

This is a refrain repeated in Christian theology from the
beginning. Christ has released us from the shackles of religious
obligation. He has liberated us from enforced codes of behavior. "It
is for freedom that Christ has set us free," says Paul. He says, "All
things are lawful, but not all things are helpful." Augustine says,
"Love, and do what you will." Martin Luther and John Calvin both
stressed that our salvation comes through *sola fide*—not through
specific actions but by faith alone.

They don't mean it, though, do they? All things are lawful.
Love and do what you will. Faith alone. Not one of them means
it, not really. Once you get them talking, it turns out they're
all pretty sure what you should and shouldn't be getting up to,
even Paul.

"Do you not know that wrongdoers will not inherit the kingdom of God? Do not be deceived! Fornicators, idolaters, adulterers,
male prostitutes, sodomites, thieves, the greedy, drunkards, revilers,
robbers—none of these will inherit the kingdom of God."

All things are lawful, but some things, it turns out, will get you
eternally jammed.[3]

In practice, every church has a vision of the moral order, some clear, some not so clear. Over the last two-thousand-plus years, some Christians have lived in voluntary poverty and some have pointed to their wealth as proof of salvation. Some have risked their lives to spread the word in hostile corners, and some have raked in big bucks preaching in the heart of town. Some have given up sex for life, some have demanded that other people give up sex of one kind or another. Some have devoted themselves to charity and good works among the poor, and some have lashed their own backs with studded whips. Some have freed slaves. Some have burned witches and infidels at the stake. Some have wrested prostitutes and addicts from the clutches of their maladjustments. Some have denigrated and persecuted Jews. And some have simply attended church on Sunday and clucked their tongues at the shenanigans of the general population.

For myself, I enjoy church a couple of times a month or so, and I'm deeply opposed to any and all shenanigans except my own, which are delightful. And a few of the other occupations listed above seem worthwhile to me in a vague sort of way. Burning witches while whipping yourself would certainly make for an interesting afternoon.

But none of this touches the meaning and purpose of my life, this writer's life. I'm a decent enough bloke, I guess, when you get me in a good mood. I can proudly say I've never been an adulterer or a male prostitute. But when I look at the rest of Paul's list of shady characters to whom paradise is banned—fornicators, idolaters, drunkards, and the rest—I seem to remember having been each of them at one time or another. And while I regret some of it, I have to admit: not all.

And honestly, even if I were better than I am, even if I had given all my earthly goods away and walked into the depths of some savage nowhere to bathe the feet of lepers with my tears, I don't think I would have been doing what I was created to do. Whereas putting a few dollars in a collection plate from time to time and trying to be nicer than I feel does not really seem like life in abundance to me. If I was not made for sainthood—and I think we can all agree I wasn't—am I just a vessel of wrath prepared for destruction?

Because—as many an angry correspondent has informed me—I call myself a Christian. More than that, I strive to follow Christ each day in every way I can. And, of course, Paul is right that bad or sinful practices are obstacles to that endeavor. But when the obstacles are cleared away, what does the endeavor itself look like? It can't just be a list of things I shouldn't do and other things I feel guilty about because I do them anyway. What more then? I want to know, need to know, because, again, it gives me so much joy when I stumble into it and get it right.

And that is—again—why it matters so much to me to know Jesus well enough that I can understand what he was actually saying.

Which is much, much harder to do than some people seem to appreciate. When I returned to the Gospels with my crummy Greek and my resolution to clear away the barnacles of tradition and traditional theology—to read Christ fresh and know him as a man—it wasn't just the Sermon on the Mount that I found odd and blurry. It was almost all blurry and all odd.

When Peter tried to walk on water, when he did walk on water, and then became afraid and began to sink beneath the waves, Jesus rebuked him and said, "Oh ye of little faith! Why did you doubt?" Was he kidding? The man walked on water for a few steps. How much faith was he supposed to have? How many steps on water have you taken? Me, not any. Is my faith too little, or is that just the way water is?

And when Jesus said, "Do not worry about what you'll eat or wear. Consider the birds of the air and the lilies of the field. The birds find food. And the lilies are clothed like Solomon in his glory." What mother with a hungry child could take such counsel? What father who has lost his job could take it?

Why did he weep at the tomb of Lazarus if he knew he was going to bring him back to life? Why did he spit on the earth to make the mud that healed a blind man? When he said, "Take up your cross," did he mean you should seek out suffering? Because that seems like a really bad idea to me. And when he said, "Give all your money to the poor," was he talking to me specifically? Because I won't and, more to the point, I don't really deep down believe I should. What did he mean by "be perfect like your father in heaven is perfect"? I sure hope it wasn't what it sounds like he meant.

Of course, I had read books and heard sermons that covered all these questions. Some of those books and sermons were good, interesting, wise. And yes, I understood the general idea that we're sinful and imperfect and the world is broken and that we need to trust him who is not sinful and not imperfect but whole.

Still, I was not satisfied. There were simply too many places in the Gospels where I could not fathom what Jesus was talking about. I had never heard anyone really engage with that—with just how weird his sayings are, how alien to life not just as we Christians live it but as we even try to live it, as we even think it is possible or useful or good to live it.

And sure, as I thought these things, I heard Paul say to me, "Who are you, O man, to talk back to God?"

But I also heard Jesus say, "I have called you friends, for everything that I learned from my Father I have made known to you."[4]

So I felt I had to talk back to him. I had to ask him some questions at least. Because I didn't feel I knew what had been made known. Not even half.

3.

Therefore, I read the Gospels again, in Greek and, following my son's advice, I stopped trying to understand Jesus' philosophy and instead tried to get to know him: who he was inside, how he saw the world, how he tried to make us see it. And that is ultimately what this book is about: the final section is my meditation on the Gospels as they spoke to me when I approached them in this way.

But on first glance, it may seem that the chapters between here and there are about things entirely unrelated. In a way, that's true. They're about literature, mostly poetry, mostly by the English Romantic poets, mostly William Wordsworth, Samuel Coleridge, and John Keats, with one chapter on the novel *Frankenstein* by their contemporary Mary Shelley. So it would not surprise me if you found yourself thinking, *Where's the Jesus here? Why am I reading this? What has this got to do with the Gospels?*

I understand that discussing these writers might seem like a peculiar path to understanding Christ. It might actually *be* a peculiar path to understanding Christ. And yet, again and again, as I reread the Gospels, it was their voices that spoke to me, their poetry that broke through the quirks and limitations of mere reason, and let me feel the savior as a presence, a man whom I might truly come to know.

Before I begin, then, I want to explain why I think this was, why I believe the life, times, thoughts, and writings of these Romantics provide a fresh and illuminating way to look at Jesus—a way to see him that I think will be inspiring not only to an admittedly offbeat individual like myself but to any believer or might-be believer who sometimes finds the religious whispers of his soul drowned out by the devices and desires of the present age.

The present age, our age, from around 1960, say, to this moment, looks uncannily like theirs, the age of the English Romantics, from about 1770 to around 1850. As the social revolution of the 1960s sought to usher in a utopia of universal peace and love, so the French Revolution of the 1770s rapidly became a search for utopian liberty, equality, and brotherhood. "We are stardust, we are golden," Joni Mitchell wrote of the youth of the 1960s, "and we've got to get ourselves back to the Garden." "Bliss was it in that dawn to be alive," wrote Wordsworth of the 1770s, "but to be young was very heaven!"[5]

These revolutions failed, as all utopian revolutions must. The tyranny inherent in their luminous philosophies worked out its conclusion in far-flung wars fought in foreign lands: the proxy battles of the Cold War for us, the Napoleonic War for my poets. When these wars were over, our countries—America, England—became the premier nations of their eras, the leaders of the free world.

But while, with the promise of utopia gone, a conservative political reaction set in, that reaction could not stop the revolution of minds. New science was undermining old beliefs. New ideas were breaking down traditions, often with shocking speed. Our nations and our times were wracked by uprisings, infighting, philosophical doubt, and political disruption. Radicals and traditionalists wrestled for control of the popular imagination.

In Romantic England, a new Christian movement called the Evangelicals began to campaign for a return to virtue and piety. At the same time, progressives began to question every assumption on which the civilization was based. Feminists sought to dismantle gender roles, sexual mores, and the institution of marriage. Reformers railed against the treatment of people of color. Historians wondered whether this mighty nation would fall like every other nation before it, and whether it ought to fall for the betterment of the greater world.

It was eerily there and then as it is here and now.

And with it all, beneath it all—to my mind, at the source of it all, then as now—were the growing doubts, first about Christianity, and then about the very existence of God. Then as now, atheism, long reviled and suppressed, became a legitimate minority view. In fact, for many intellectuals—then as now—the central principle of the age was unbelief.

Unbelief—this was and is at the core of our divisions because faith was and is at the core of Western culture.

For the civilization once known as Christendom, the life and ministry of Jesus was a cosmic watershed, after which nothing was the same. It was like a nuclear blast, only spiritual. A blinding light, at first, in the midst of which the old ideas were vaporized. Then mad mutations: miracles and revelations and speaking in tongues. Next came the gradual irradiation of the world, strange changes in mankind until, after slow centuries, everything was different. Worship abandoned its endless sacrifices. Kings perceived a limit to their powers. The value of mercy, charity, and agape-love claimed priority over honor, vengeance, and pride. Women began to be valued as persons. Persons were seen to have natural rights. The conscience of each individual acquired new authority, sometimes even authority over the law. Time became a matter of before and after Bethlehem, until every Western soul—every thought it had, every vision, every story it told, every metaphor it made, language itself—became a Christian instrument.

For a Westerner, there is no walking away from the Christian mindset. It is the skin we wear, the air we breathe, a world that travels with us. Even when we reject God it is a rejection of the Christian God specifically. In his hilarious novel *Catch-22*, Joseph Heller has a character cry out in anguish, "The God I don't believe in is a good God, a just God, a merciful God."[6] Even in his unbelief, Western man sees through the eyes of a believer.

All the same, for the Romantics—and isn't it true for us as well?—old Christendom was in ruins. Modernity had disenchanted the human territory. The earth had ceased to appear a place of angels and demons, miracles and magic, with a heaven painted on the sky above and a hell in the hidden pits and mountains underground. The beliefs of the religion had become conflated with the ignorant superstitions of the centuries through which it had passed so that when science undermined those superstitions, it seemed to undermine the religion itself. The church had become oppressive and corrupt so that thinking people were estranged from it. For nearly three centuries, the struggle between Catholics and Protestants had been marked by unthinkable acts of war and persecution that discredited the believers' claims to be followers of the Prince of Peace. "Christians . . . have inflicted far greater severities on each other than they had experienced from the zeal of infidels," as Edward

Gibbon wrote in his *Decline and Fall of the Roman Empire*, first published in 1776.

The problem the Romantics faced, says the great critic Jacques Barzun, "was to create a new world on the ruins of the old."[7]

But they could not unshape themselves. They could not stop being what eighteen hundred years of Christian civilization had made them.

So rather than building their new world from scratch, in the words of scholar M. H. Abrams, the Romantics began to rediscover "traditional concepts, schemes, and values which had been based on the relation of the Creator to his creature and creation,"[8] but to reframe those ideas as part of "the human mind or consciousness and its transactions with nature." Abrams calls this *natural supernaturalism*, an attempt to reinvent the miraculous Gospels out of the human experience of the natural world.

This may not have been good theology, but they were not theologians, they were poets. And in trying to do what they did, I believe they stumbled on something that is at the center of who Jesus was, what he knew and wanted us to know: the world of angels and demons, the landscape alive with miracles and magic, the life that promises heaven and puts us at risk of hell—these are not illusions from some implausible phantasmagoria that stands in opposition to reason and science and everyday experience. They are this world, this landscape, this life we are living right here, right now.

In short, the Romantics looked at godless nature, and Christian truth looked back. This, I think, is why C. S. Lewis, like so many others, found the poetry of Wordsworth, for instance, a stepping-stone to faith. "For some souls I believe, for my own I remember, Wordsworthian contemplation can be the first and lowest form of recognition that there is something outside ourselves which demands reverence . . . For 'the man coming up from below' the Wordsworthian experience is an advance. Even if he goes no further he has escaped the worst arrogance of materialism: if he goes on he will be converted."[9]

It worked for Lewis. If it comes to that, it worked for Wordsworth, who himself became a Christian in the end.

In a way, then, the project of the English Romantics resembled my own project in rereading the Gospels. The Romantics set aside all religious precepts and traditions in order to see things anew. And in an age that was much like ours—an age of unbelief—these genius poets, in works of spectacular depth and beauty, in ways that were often unintentional—either accidentally or guided by a hand they could not perceive—blazed a literary trail back from the ruins of the old faith—from the smoking shambles left by human superstition, corruption, and violence—toward the original vision that Christ delivered not only in the Sermon on the Mount but in all the works and words of that invisible biography that hovers in the credal silence between his miraculous birth and his suffering death. Mostly without seeking to, mostly without meaning to, these poets rediscovered what is provable in the living of it: that the deepest experience of human existence, the most creative, the most joyful, and surely the most true is the experience taught to us by the incarnate Word of God and bought for us by his crucifixion and resurrection.

The first part of this book, then, discusses the Romantics in terms of the problems they were facing, the symptoms of increasing godlessness: moral relativism, a disbelief in objective truth, a confusion about gender roles, and the delusion that the sinful human world can be perfected by deconstructing its traditions and reforming them through radical politics. They are problems a modern reader should find familiar.

The second part of the book looks at the ways the poets moved beyond these symptoms and began the business of reconstructing and salvaging man's instinctive knowledge of the supernatural, his sense that he has a soul, that there is a life beyond life, that the seemingly indifferent universe is, in fact, a personal creator's act of love. It is the wisdom of the ancients translated for the modern mind, the timeless truth restated in startlingly original terms.

The final part is my rereading of the Gospels informed by that reconstructed wisdom: the life and words, miracles and resurrection of Jesus seen as the surest guide to the deepest knowledge of reality.

In my memoir about my conversion, *The Great Good Thing: A Secular Jew Comes to Faith in Christ*, I wrote about how it was literature that led me to Christianity in the first place. My childhood search for models of manhood had given me a love for American tough guy fiction, especially the great detective novels of Raymond Chandler and Dashiell Hammett. The under-themes of knighthood and quest in those novels caused me to delve into the Arthurian legends, and in those legends, the effects of Christian faith were everywhere apparent. So I read the Gospels (with what tragic-hilarious results you'll have to read my memoir to find out). And as I discovered my vocation as a writer, as I educated myself in the Western canon, it became vividly apparent to me that the poet William Blake was right when he said, "The Old and New Testaments are the Great Code of Art."[10]

In that code and in that art are embedded that portion of the Western vision that is the simple truth not just for westerners but for humankind altogether. And it came to seem to me, as a matter of simple integrity, that I had to believe in the Singer if I wanted to sing that true song.

It made perfect sense, therefore, that when I returned to Jesus searching for a deeper understanding of his words, he sent me back to literature—to the poetry I loved most—so that it could explain him to me anew. To paraphrase the lines of T. S. Eliot, a modern Christian poet deeply influenced by the Romantic tradition, the end of all my exploring was to arrive where I had started and to know the place for the first time.

I hope that others will find what I found: that that journey—that literary journey of the Romantics through an age of unbelief back to the entryway of faith—is nothing less than the journey home.

PART 1

THE PROBLEMS OF A GODLESS WORLD

CHAPTER 1

THE IMMORTAL EVENING

The Spiritual Hinge of History

One cold Sunday in the Christmas season, 1817, Benjamin Robert Haydon had four friends to his rooms for dinner. Fierce-faced and bald-headed, Haydon was, to use a fine old word, a cockalorum—a self-important little man. He wanted desperately to be the greatest historical painter in English history. He prayed to God to make it so. He tried to will it so himself. He tried to force the world to declare it was. But it never was. Hard as he labored to wrest vast biblical and classical scenes out of his canvases, he could not bring them off the surface into life. His sense of perspective was second rate. His faces were mostly inanimate. He "had utterly mistaken his vocation," Charles Dickens said of him after his death.[1] His work was "quite marvelous in its badness."[2]

All that said, he was a good friend: a supportive mentor, a wonderful dinner-party companion, and a terrific conversationalist. He was full of intellectual passion. He knew about everything and could talk about anything in English, French, or Italian. "One enjoys his hearty, joyous laugh," said the essayist William Hazlitt, a close observer of the times. "It sets one upon one's legs as it were better than a glass of champagne, for one is delighted to meet such a cheery spirit, in the saddening depression that broods over the hypocrisy and despotism of the world."[3]

Haydon's main purpose in arranging this dinner was to bring together two of the greatest literary men of a remarkably great literary era. One was the famous poet William Wordsworth. He was almost fifty at this time, but twenty years before, he had revolutionized English verse with a collection called *Lyrical Ballads*, written in collaboration with another great, Samuel Taylor Coleridge. Haydon had arranged for him to dine this evening with an aspiring poet named John Keats. Just twenty-two years old, Keats was no one now, and in little more than three years, he would be dead and gone. But between this night and then, he would prove himself the purest poetic talent England had produced since William Shakespeare.

Wordsworth and Keats had met for the first time just a few days before. That meeting—and this one and others that followed through the winter—would begin to change the course of Keats's thought, which, in turn, would change the history of English poetry.

For a long time before they met, Keats had revered Wordsworth. About a year before, he had written a lovely sonnet about him—about him and about the excitement and promise of the extraordinary moment in which they were living.

He had composed the sonnet after a visit with Haydon. The painter had known Keats only a short time then, but from the very first he recognized the young poet for the genius he was and brought him into his circle. Keats was an appealing character, very short—only about "five feet high," he wrote of himself once[4]—but handsome and decent hearted and vibrant with youth and virile energy, lofty ambition, and high ideals.

One night that November, Haydon invited him to his studio to meet Hazlitt. The essayist was sitting for a portrait that would be included in yet another of Haydon's big, bad paintings, *Christ's Entry into Jerusalem*. As Haydon painted and Hazlitt sat and Keats looked on, the talk among the men was all about the spirit of the age, the ferment of creative brilliance in English arts and letters everywhere, and the role of poetry in creating a new consciousness for humankind.

The talk left Keats inspired. He was still uncertain of his gift, still struggling to find his voice, but he was so hungry to do work that would place him "among the English poets" that his imagination was ignited by the delicious torment of the era's possibilities. Was it possible that he—the unknown son of a stableman—could become one of the titans of this titanic time?

As he walked home that evening, he began to compose:

> Great spirits now on earth are sojourning;
> He of the cloud, the cataract, the lake,
> Who on Helvellyn's summit, wide awake,
> Catches his freshness from Archangel's wing . . .

That—"He of the cloud," and so on—was Wordsworth. Helvellyn was the tallest peak in the Lake District, where Wordsworth lived and, apparently, collaborated with the archangels to write his poetry. He and Coleridge and also Robert Southey had become known as the Lake Poets or the Lake School, or sometimes, dismissively, the Lakers.

After praising Wordsworth, Keats's sonnet went on to mention the political essayist Leigh Hunt and then—with more of friendship than artistic taste—Haydon himself. At last it concluded on a high note of triumph:

> And other spirits there are standing apart
> Upon the forehead of the age to come;
> These, these will give the world another heart
> And other pulses. Hear ye not the hum
> Of mighty workings in the human mart?
> Listen awhile, ye nations, and be dumb.[5]

Keats sent the sonnet to Haydon, and when Haydon wrote to say that he would pass the poem along to Wordsworth himself, Keats was thrilled. "The idea of your sending it to Wordsworth put me out of breath," he wrote back. "You know with what Reverence—I would send my Well wishes to him."[6]

Unfortunately, however, the first meeting between the two poets did not go well.

It was a year after the Great Spirits sonnet, just a few days before Haydon's Christmas dinner. Wordsworth was in London for a few months on business. He was staying at the home of his wife's cousin, Thomas Monkhouse, in the West End. Haydon walked Keats over and Keats, he said, was glowing with "the purest, the most unalloyed pleasure" at the prospect of meeting his hero.[7]

Wordsworth greeted the young man graciously enough, but he was, all the same, an intimidating figure.

For one thing, his achievement as an artist was epic. In the words of T. S. Eliot, "The great poet, in writing himself, writes his time."[8] Wordsworth and Coleridge had produced *Lyrical Ballads* just as young Europe's high hopes for the French Revolution were devolving into disappointment and revulsion at the terror and war that followed. As the atrocities of Stalin would in the 1930s and '40s, the events of the 1780s and '90s forced honest thinkers to confront the failure of their utopian politics. Night had fallen forever on the past behind them, but what they'd thought was sunrise up ahead turned out just to be blood on the horizon. Which way then did the future lie?

As Jacques Barzun put it, "Even before the Revolution, which may be taken as the outward sign of an inward decay, it was no longer possible to think, act, write, or paint as if the old forms still had life."[9] In *Lyrical Ballads*, Wordsworth and Coleridge had reinvented English poetry for this new age. In doing so, they had helped reinvent the Western mind itself. They had given "the world another heart, and other pulses," just as Keats had written.

And there was also this: Wordsworth was very good at being Wordsworth. He knew how to live into his own magnificence. Tall and imposing, with solemn, noble features under thinning brown hair, he was so self-possessed in presence and so majestic in thought and utterance that he could sometimes seem almost otherworldly, an immortal in his mortal moment, which in fact he was.

Plus, he was often irritable when he was in London. I've sometimes wondered if, for all his display of eminence, he felt insecure when he left the Lakes and came to the big city. Maybe here, among urban sophisticates, the country dweller was less certain of his own reputation. His reviews from the intellectual establishment had always been mixed, at best. And recently, too, he had begun to feel his powers fading. Maybe a touch of uncertainty led him to overdo his protective aura of self-importance from time to time.

And finally, he was undergoing a slow but profound metamorphosis in his philosophical outlook. He had been a fashionable radical in his youth. He was damned as a conservative now. He had been a "semi-atheist," as Coleridge once put it, but he was now on his way to becoming a Christian.[10] He had good reasons for these changes, but having gone through them myself, I know: it can be easy to overshoot the center for a while. Wordsworth these days could occasionally seem rigid and reactionary and unpleasantly pious. He was a good man, a loving husband, brother, father, and friend. He had a fondness for children and a heart for the poor. But nowadays sometimes, his grand persona could shade over the line of grandeur and he could come across, to say it bluntly, as a bit of a pompous ass.

~e⁊

So anyway, Haydon brought Keats for a visit. The great man and his young worshiper chatted for a little while with the painter looking on. Then Wordsworth asked Keats what he had been writing lately. Haydon piped up that Keats had just finished "an exquisite ode to Pan."[11] He urged him to recite it then and there.

The ode was part of Keats's first long poem *Endymion*, which begins with the famous lines:

> A thing of beauty is a joy for ever:
> Its loveliness increases; it will never
> Pass into nothingness . . .[12]

Keats stood to deliver. We can only imagine how nervous he must have been. He knew that, in writing such a long piece, he had taken on more than he was ready for. There was greatness in it here and there, but there were great flaws too, and he was painfully aware of all of them. Still, he began to recite his verse in front of Wordsworth, pacing back and forth across the room. His voice fell into a sort of chant, as it often did when he recited. Haydon looked on and listened, enthralled. When Keats finished, Haydon felt as if he had heard "a young Apollo," the god of poetry himself.[13]

But Wordsworth was not impressed.

Keats waited for the great man's verdict on his work, trembling, Haydon said later, "like the String of a Lyre, when it has been touched."

Then Wordsworth remarked dismissively: "A very pretty piece of paganism."

"Keats felt it deeply," Haydon wrote. "He never forgave him."[14] It was the beginning of Keats's disillusionment with his hero—an awakening that would free him to do more original work and to bring Wordsworth's new vision of man to a spiritual fulfillment beyond Wordsworth's poetic power.

Nevertheless, for now Keats was no one and Wordsworth was a great man. Keats showed up eagerly at Haydon's rooms that Sunday for Christmas dinner.

Thomas Monkhouse—a cousin of Wordsworth's wife—would also be there. In fact, being at that dinner is what history mostly remembers him for. Then there was Charles Lamb.

Lamb has been called "the most lovable figure in English

literature."[15] He probably was, but what a tragic character he was too. He was in his early forties, with deep, sad, distant eyes and the mournful, sensitive features of an impoverished parson. He was from modest circumstances originally, the son of a lawyer's factotum. He had tried in his youth to make a go of writing poetry, fiction, and plays. Then, about ten years back, he had finally achieved success with a children's book he cowrote with his older sister, Mary, *Tales from Shakespeare*. He was now in the process of becoming one of the excellent essayists in an age of excellent essays.

And like Haydon, he knew everyone. He and his sister both did. Artistic London loved to gather around the two of them for conversational salons. Charles especially was beloved for his impish wit and his gentle, childlike manner. Almost every sentence out of his mouth was a quip, and hilarious.

But he was also a drunk and a man of sorrows. And with good reason.

His mother had been a cold and querulous woman. His sister Mary—eleven years his senior—was of a sweet, nurturing disposition and had supplied whatever mothering Charles received. But when he was seven, Charles was sent to Christ's Hospital, a charity boarding school of exceptional cruelty. It was there he began a lifelong friendship with his fellow student Coleridge. But whereas Coleridge went on to Cambridge, Lamb, hampered by a lifelong stutter, was left behind to become trapped in a boring job in the accounting office of the British East India Company.

He was frustrated in his career. And he was frustrated in his love life when the woman he courted for years rejected him for someone else. Finally, at only twenty years old, the mild-mannered man went mad. He grew violent with his family and fell under the delusion he was the tragic hero of a popular play. He was sent away and spent six weeks in an asylum.

After he returned, his home life began to deteriorate. His father descended into senility. His mother became paralyzed by arthritis and spent all day sitting in her chair griping and making biting remarks. His brother John, who had moved away to work as a lawyer's assistant, was injured in an accident, so he returned home too. And the burden of all this fell on his sister Mary, who nursed them, and also had to nurse her aging aunt Sarah, and also had to earn her living as a seamstress, and also had to train a little girl as an apprentice.

With that sweet, nurturing disposition of hers, Mary bore these tasks dutifully—until one day, she didn't.

That was what Charles would later come to call the "day of horrors."[16]

Maybe it was some syndrome that ran in the family, or maybe it was their upbringing or just the pressures she was under, but in any case, Mary's mind began to crack, just as Charles's had.

She showed signs of violent anger. It got so bad that on the morning of September 22, 1796, Charles went out to fetch the family doctor. When he arrived at the doctor's house, the doctor was out. Charles went in search of him through the neighborhood. He couldn't find him.

Meanwhile, back home, tensions began to rise. Mary's young apprentice made some mistake and Mary lost her temper with her. Mary's mother, carping from her chair as always, began to scold Mary for mistreating the girl.

Mary broke.

One of Lamb's biographers, Sarah Burton, describes the scene that Charles found as he was arriving home.[17]

"He may have heard the apprentice girl's scream . . . Perhaps he collided with the child in the hallway as she fled, speechless with terror. Charles pushed the parlour-door open warily. The only sound was that of a man sobbing. As the door swung open, inch by inch the scale of the disaster was revealed. Furniture was overturned; the floor was littered with food, broken crockery, and cutlery. His mother, father and sister were covered in blood . . .

"His father, bleeding from his head was weeping. His aunt, white with shock, seemed rooted to the spot."

And Lamb's mother, covered with gore, was splayed in her armchair, lifeless. Mary stood over her, "her face and clothes spattered with blood." She was still holding the carving knife with which she had stabbed her mother to death.

In the aftermath of the butchery, the coroner ruled Mary insane. She was put in an asylum, but she seemed to recover quickly. After only six months, she was released.

With that, she and Charles began their long and difficult life in tandem. Whenever Mary was free, she kept his house and took care of him. But every year or so, her mind would crumble again. Then, holding hands and weeping, off the two would walk together to another asylum, where she would be put away until she was well.

So yes, Lamb was lovable, gentle, childlike, and a witty fellow. But he was also a drunk and a man of sorrows.

He would be the fifth at Haydon's dinner party.

⇛

Haydon and Wordsworth and Keats and Monkhouse and Lamb. The guests arrived around 3:30, which is near dusk on a December day in London. They assembled to dine in Haydon's "painting room."

There was a sixth presence there as well. Propped on an easel, lit by firelight as the winter sun went down, Haydon's painting, *Christ's Entry into Jerusalem*, served as a backdrop for the gathering. This was the same painting Haydon had been working on a year before when he and Hazlitt and Keats had talked. He had been laboring on it for three years, in fact, and it would be another three years before he was finished with it.

It was—it is—a crowded, monumental scene. Here into the city comes the savior of the world, riding on a donkey as the Old Testament prophet Zechariah foretold:

> Rejoice greatly, O daughter Zion!
> Shout aloud, O daughter Jerusalem!
> Lo, your king comes to you;
> triumphant and victorious is he,
> humble and riding on a donkey,
> on a colt, the foal of a donkey.

The Messiah's head is swathed in radiance. His hands are lifted in blessing. The rejoicing people throng the roadway to welcome him. They gaze at the Christ in wonder as he passes. One woman shields her eyes, as if blinded by the light of his presence. Another spreads her yellow mantle on the road to smooth his way. One man falls to his knees. A turbaned Lazarus, recently brought back from the dead, prostrates himself.

Among the crowd, there are faces modeled on famous men

of the new age and of the last. Off to one side, in the shadow of some palm trees, there stands Wordsworth, his head bowed in devotion, his hand resting on his heart. Isaac Newton, the source and symbol of modern science, stands beside him. Newton, who was a Christian, stares at the scene intently as if trying to capture every detail in his mind. The Enlightenment philosopher Voltaire is with them too. One of the French thinkers who had paved the way for the revolution, and a harsh critic of Christianity and the Catholic Church, Voltaire is sneering as the Christ rides by.

Behind these three, a man is shouting something to another man who turns back to hear him. The shouting man is Keats.

So the poets were there twice that evening, at two of history's spiritual hinges, once in these London rooms in an era of revolution, and once on the road to Jerusalem, watching Jesus ride past them into the days of his passion.

~e

The dinner got off to a delightful start. Wordsworth, as usual, began declaiming with ponderous authority. He recited Milton so solemnly it sounded to Haydon like a combination of the funeral bell of St. Paul's Cathedral and the music of Handel—the "Hallelujah Chorus" perhaps. Wordsworth delivered some sonorous Virgil too as Keats and the others looked on admiring and inspired.

But they didn't let Wordsworth cow them into silence. They held their own. The discussion was lively, ranging not only over Milton and Virgil but over Homer and Shakespeare—and Voltaire too. Wordsworth, probably looking at the image of himself with Voltaire in the painting, had the daring to declare the revolutionary Frenchman a dullard.

All the while, of course, Lamb was hammering the wine hard. It made him merry and mischievous. He started to tease Wordsworth and interrupt his high rhetoric with sarcastic cracks. Wordsworth, since a bad night of drunkenness back in his Cambridge days, didn't drink very much, only the occasional glass of ale. Keats, whose health was always fragile, mostly tried to restrict himself to a couple of glasses of wine. But Lamb was growing increasingly hilarious, and the poets couldn't resist him. Even Wordsworth's oratory started to give way to laughter—which was a delight to everyone.

Lamb rose from his seat to deliver a zany speech in which he voted Haydon absent and drank his health. Then he started in on Wordsworth again.

"Now," he said, "you old lake poet, you rascally poet, why do you call Voltaire dull?"

The others quickly rose to Wordsworth's defense. You know, they said, when you thought about it, you could see how there was a state of mind in which Voltaire might be dull.

"Well," said Lamb, raising yet another glass, "here's Voltaire— the messiah of the French nation, and a very proper one too."

As Lamb recharged his glass, he nodded toward the painting flickering in the firelight. A religious man himself, he started to tease Haydon mercilessly for including Newton in a gospel scene.

"Newton was a fellow who believed nothing unless it was as clear as the three sides of a triangle," Lamb said.

Keats jokingly joined in. Newton, he declared, had purged the world of enchantment. Where were the satyrs and fauns that used to haunt the forests? Where were the dreams and speculations that entered a man's imagination as he lay in the grass and watched the white doves flying through the white clouds? Newton, said Keats, "had destroyed all the poetry of the rainbow by reducing it to the prismatic colors."

Well, as Lamb saw it, this called for another toast!

"Newton's health and confusion to mathematics," he cried.[18]

And they all drank.

⁂

The evening wore on. They adjourned to another room for tea: light snacks, more drinking. After-dinner guests began to arrive. There was John Landseer, a talented landscape engraver whose sons studied art with Haydon. He was a lively, smart, sarcastic man, but almost completely deaf.

And there was "Richer," Joseph Ritchie, a young surgeon. He had wanted to be a writer and still enjoyed hanging out with literary types. Ritchie had recently met Keats's brothers in Paris, and was already convinced that Keats himself would become "the great luminary of the age to come."[19] He was also in awe of Wordsworth's work and compared it to Milton's. He must've been delighted to be among this company.

In fact, this was a good time for Ritchie in general. Once he had realized he had no talent for writing, he had been casting around for some way to make himself known, as he put it. Just recently, he had been placed at the head of a planned expedition to Africa, funded by the British government. The expedition's goal was to discover the source of the River Niger and trace its tortuous meanderings to the sea.

"I have never been so happy in my life as since it has been finally determined on," he said.

Haydon introduced Ritchie to the group as "a gentleman

going to Africa." Lamb, by this time, was reaching the dozy stage of drunkenness. At first, nodding in his chair, he seemed to pay no attention to the new arrival. Keats, on the other hand, was always interested in groundbreaking discoveries and explorations. Poignantly, he made Ritchie promise to take a copy of *Endymion* with him and "fling it into the midst" of the sands of the Sahara Desert.

Then, suddenly, Lamb sat up and roared out, "Which is the gentleman we are going to lose?"[20]

Why, this called for a toast! Everyone laughed and drank to the health of the doomed man—including the doomed man himself.

Two years later, with his expedition stranded in what is now Libya, tangled in red tape and bogged down by his own tactical errors, Ritchie died of fever in the desert town of Murzuk.

❧

There was one more guest who arrived around that time: John Kingston, a comptroller of stamps.

Kingston had turned up at Haydon's door earlier that day. Haydon didn't know the man at all, but Kingston had somehow found out about the planned dinner. He proceeded to wangle an invitation to the after-dinner party. Kingston said he'd met Keats once. He said he loved Wordsworth's poetry and had "often had a correspondence" with him.[21] Haydon was annoyed by the man's presumption, but Kingston seemed like a gentleman, so he finally gave in and told him he could come.

But there was a problem—an awkwardness—in Kingston's joining the gathering. Something Haydon hadn't quite thought through.

Despite his growing fame, Wordsworth was always in need of money. There were women who depended on him: his sister, Dorothy, his wife, Mary, her sister Sarah sometimes too. He had three children still living, the oldest only fourteen. There were bills to pay.

He had a patron, Lake Country peer Lord Lonsdale. But Wordsworth had been reluctant to accept a charitable pension from him. Ultimately, though, he had accepted a different gift: a government job in Lord Lonsdale's control. Wordsworth was now distributor of stamps for the county of Westmoreland. That's how he made his living.

Legal documents needed government stamps in those days—it was a way of collecting taxes on them. You would buy the stamps from a local tradesman. Wordsworth's job was to make sure the stamps were distributed around the county and to collect the money for them after they were sold. It wasn't a sinecure. It was real work. It involved a lot of travel and record keeping and took up a lot of time. Wordsworth, being Wordsworth, took the job seriously and did it responsibly and well.

This made Kingston, essentially, his civil service superior. So yes, it was true Wordsworth had received occasional official "correspondence" from him. But it was also true that he had no idea who the man was.

Lamb was dozing by the fire now. Keats and Ritchie were at the bookshelves, examining Haydon's library. Monkhouse and Landseer, the deaf engraver, were still there, chatting. Haydon briefly introduced Kingston to the room but forgot to mention who he was.

Kingston turned out to be a nice, mild-mannered fellow, but he was a bit of a weak character and way out of his element here.

He talked too much: he clearly wanted to be part of the evening's high literary conversation. Just as clearly, he didn't have what it took to join in.

After a while, the comptroller found a seat next to Wordsworth. He looked down to gather his thoughts. Then he looked up and said to the poet, "Don't you think, sir, Milton was a great genius?"

Keats exchanged a glance with Haydon. Wordsworth could only look at Kingston, at a complete loss as to how to reply.

Suddenly, Lamb came out of his snooze. He cocked his head at the comptroller and said, "Pray, sir, did you say Milton was a great genius?"

"No, sir," Kingston replied, "I asked Mr. Wordsworth if he were not."

"Oh," said Lamb, "then you are a silly fellow."

"Charles! My dear Charles!" said Wordsworth, forcing down a chuckle.

But it was too late. Lamb had already gone back to sleep.

There was a deadly pause.

Then the comptroller said to Wordsworth, "Don't you think Newton a great genius?"

Keats started to crack up. He buried his face in one of Haydon's books. Ritchie let a short laugh break out of him before he could stop it.

Wordsworth was speechless. He seemed to be asking himself, *Who on earth is this person?*

Then, all at once, Lamb was wide awake. He sprang up out of his chair and grabbed a nearby candle. He held the flame over Kingston's head and said, "Sir, will you allow me to look at your phrenological development?"

Keats, Ritchie, and Haydon all had to hide their faces as they fought down laughter. Landseer couldn't hear what was going on and was leaning forward, baffled, his hand to his ear.

Kingston started to respond, but Lamb turned his back on him and skipped back to his chair, singing, "Diddle diddle dumpling, my son John, went to bed with his breeches on." He sank into his seat again.

Confused, Kingston tried to smile, tried to be polite without losing his dignity. He was now finally beginning to realize that Wordsworth hadn't the faintest idea who he was. He chuckled, thinking all he had to do was clear that up and his presence would start to make sense to one and all.

He said, "I have had the honor of some correspondence with you, Mr. Wordsworth."

"With me, sir?" said Wordsworth. "Not that I remember."

"Don't you, sir? I—am a comptroller of stamps."

Absolute silence. Kingston sat back with a look of satisfaction. Wordsworth stared at him helplessly, trying to come up with a response.

Lamb started singing again: "Hey diddle diddle, the cat and the fiddle."

"My dear Charles!" Wordsworth said.

"Diddle diddle dumpling, my son John," Lamb sang. He jumped from his chair and grabbed the candle again, crying, "Do let me have another look at that gentleman's organs!"

That was it. Keats and Haydon could no longer control themselves. They grabbed Lamb under the arms and hustled him back into the painting room. They quickly shut the door and then exploded with laughter.

Kingston, of course, was deeply offended. Monkhouse realized something had to be done. He followed the others into the painting room and tried to convince Lamb to go home and sleep it off.

Haydon had to get back to the party and restore good order. He and Keats got themselves under control and returned to the tea room, where they tried to soothe Kingston's feelings. That was just Lamb, they said. That was just the way Lamb was.

But all the while, they could hear Monkhouse struggling with Lamb behind the painting-room door and Lamb shouting, "Who is that fellow? Allow me to see his organs once more!"

Finally—finally—Monkhouse persuaded Lamb to let him take him home. That ended the chaos. Haydon managed to calm Kingston down, though clearly the comptroller had taken a blow to his dignity. Wordsworth may have felt his own dignity had suffered some too. After all, he had been demoted in a single moment from literary giant to civil service underling.

In the end, though, Kingston really was a decent fellow. He let himself be mollified. They all sat down to supper together, and good feelings were restored.

—⁓

"It was indeed an immortal evening," Haydon wrote later. "A night worthy of the Elizabethan age."[22]

It was too. Whole books have been written about just that dinner. No biography of Wordsworth or Keats is complete without a description of it. Not only does it serve as a delightful dramatization of how mighty ideas are carried in the minds of flawed, tragic, and wackily absurd individuals, but somehow too it seems to touch on almost every theme and trouble of the age. The recitation of Milton and the discussion of Voltaire speak of the tragic disappointment of utopian radicalism. The toast to Newton hints at the challenges and limitations of science and reason. The interplay between Wordsworth and Keats highlights the poetic search for a new human consciousness, a fresh understanding of the meaning and purpose of man.

And the painting, standing on its easel, catching the firelight—*Christ's Entry into Jerusalem*, the beginning of the end of the gospel story—seems, to me at least, to suggest what lay at the bottom of it all, the source of the mysteries these men were confronting, the reason these problems were crying to be solved.

In the painting as in the moment—as indeed in our present day—the time could be seen approaching when faith would fail and Christ would be banished from the world.

CHAPTER 2

WHO'S THERE?

Hamlet *and the*
Problem of Unbelief

A few days after the Immortal Evening, on the last day of 1817, Haydon knelt in prayer. He prayed for his painting, *Christ's Entry into Jerusalem*. He prayed that God might allow him to "conceive and execute such a head of Christ as would impress the Christian world."[1]

The answer to his prayer was no. The head of Jesus in *Christ's Entry* is awful: bland and wooden, his expression more supercilious than holy. Nevertheless, the picture had a successful showing in the Great Room of the Egyptian Hall, an exhibition center in Piccadilly. A large crowd of paying customers turned out to see it. It was the high point of Haydon's career.

In the end, though, the picture didn't sell. Haydon blamed this on the influential Royal Academy of Arts. He was forever feuding with them over their prejudice against the sort of grand historical painting he preferred. They responded by criticizing his work. Haydon felt this ruined the picture's chances with buyers.

The failure to sell the painting hit him hard. He was irresponsible with money, always in debt. Now his debts grew worse—so much worse that, a few years later, he was carted away to debtor's prison. The painting was finally sold off by the sheriff for 220 pounds. The frame alone had cost a hundred.

"Of what use is my Genius—to myself or others?" he wrote in his despair. "It has brought me in prison . . . I am ruined!"[2]

That was in 1824. He struggled on for twenty more years, making his living mostly as a lecturer, trying to promote his monumental style of work to anyone who would listen. But his reputation as an artist continued to decline.

In 1846, now sixty and still crushed by debt, he decided to make one last attempt at a comeback. Again, he rented a room at the Egyptian Hall for a show—although not the Great Room this time, a smaller one downstairs. One of the paintings he put on display was *The Banishment of Aristides*. In its composition—a lofty central figure mobbed on a city street—it is a pitifully inept reworking of the already inept *Christ's Entry*. Clearly, Haydon was trying to recapture his lost glory days, such as they were.

The upstairs rooms of the Egyptian Hall, meanwhile, were being rented by American showman P. T. Barnum. Barnum was touring Europe with his latest offbeat attraction, General Tom Thumb. Thumb was a dwarf, less than three feet tall. Barnum had taught him to sing and dance and do impersonations. His European tour was a sensation, including two shows before Queen Victoria.

When the doors to the Egyptian Hall were opened, the crowds

poured in just as they had for *Christ's Entry*. Thousands of people of every age and rank and fashion fought each other to be first through the door. But this time, as it turned out, they weren't there to see Haydon's work. They didn't even pause to glance into the little room where Haydon's *Banishment of Aristides* hung. Instead, they immediately hurried up the stairs to get a gander at the singing and dancing dwarf. In one week, twelve thousand people came to see Tom Thumb. Over the same time, Haydon recorded 133½ visitors for his artwork. The half was a little girl.

The humiliation was more than Haydon could bear. A few months later, he made his will. He went to the gun shop and bought a brace of pistols. After a long night pacing the floor of his painting room and scribbling in his diary, he waited for his wife and daughter to leave the house. Then he shot himself in the head. Even that was a failure. The bullet was deflected by his skull. It only dazed him. He staggered blindly around the room. Finally, he seized hold of a razor and hacked away savagely at his throat. At last he collapsed in a puddle of his own blood.

He left behind a lachrymose epitaph which he asked to have carved on his tombstone: "Here lieth the body of Benjamin Robert Haydon . . . who, in a struggle to make the People, the Legislature, the Nobility, and the Sovereign of England give due dignity and rank to the highest art . . . fell Victim to his ardor and love of country; and evidence that to seek the benefit of your Country by telling Truth to Power, is a crime that can only be expiated by the ruin and destruction of the Man who is so patriotic and so imprudent."[3]

Well, no. That isn't actually what happened.

Haydon had not only, as Dickens said, "mistaken his vocation," he had misjudged his era altogether. Even if he had had the talent to do what he was trying to do, he still might have ended badly. The age of the classical, the epic, the grandly religious in art was passing away. Already, painter J. M. W. Turner was moving to the very edge of impressionism. His landscapes existed at the nexus where object and observer meet. They weren't landscapes at all, really. They were merely images of light striking the mind. Soon, the subject of art would no longer be the reality we see around us but vision itself, not the grand stage of outer actions but the inner experience of man. With the coming of Romanticism—to paraphrase the title of another book by M. H. Abrams, *The Mirror and the Lamp*—the role of the artist was no longer, as Hamlet said, "to hold the mirror up to nature" but to illuminate nature with the lamp of the artist's mind and its perceptions.

But this approach created a problem, a philosophical difficulty —*the* philosophical difficulty, when you come to think about it.

When artists stopped holding the mirror up to nature, when they held the mirror instead to the mind of man, they were essentially holding a mirror up to a mirror. For man to see only what man sees is to see endless reflections of himself, empty of certainty and of certain meaning. As one of the greatest of the Romantic poets, William Blake, put it, "The eye altering, alters all."[4] So if all we know of reality is what we perceive in our minds, and if our minds are hampered by limited perceptions, and our perceptions are distorted by feelings and prejudices and delusions, how can we know the true nature of things? If all we really believe in is the inside of our own heads, how can we know reality is real at all?

This was not a new question. It was the question Pontius Pilate posed to Christ at his trial: What is truth? Christ said that *he* was—he was truth—that he testified to the truth and everyone who belonged to the truth listened to his voice.

On Christ's reply, the West had built a church and the church had helped form a civilization. As long as westerners believed in that reply, believed in Christ and his church, the civilization stood on solid ground or seemed to. But once faith in Christ was gone, only Pilate's question remained.

What is truth?

That is the central problem of unbelief.

⁃ↄ

It was 1867—exactly fifty years after the Immortal Evening—when Matthew Arnold published the poem "Dover Beach," lamenting the passing of the West's religion.

> The Sea of Faith
> Was once . . . at the full, and round earth's shore
> Lay like the folds of a bright girdle furled.
> But now I only hear
> Its melancholy, long, withdrawing roar,
> Retreating, to the breath
> Of the night-wind, down the vast edges drear
> And naked shingles of the world.[5]

But the rise of atheism was inherent in European culture from the moment in 1517—exactly three hundred years before the Immortal Evening—when Martin Luther posted his Ninety-Five Theses on the door of All Saints' Church in Wittenberg, Germany, and began the Reformation, the end of Rome's monopoly on religious truth.

⸺ℓꜱ

In a world grown increasingly empty of faith, many people no longer understand the depth of the division between Catholic and Protestant, but for those who truly believe, the trauma of the shattering of the One True Religion is still with us. There have been evenings when Catholic and Protestant friends gathered on my patio for drinks, cigars, and conversation when I feared to go inside and refresh the pretzel bowl lest the Thirty Years' War break out again in my absence. I figured I would head for the kitchen with my guests debating the perpetual virginity of Mary and return to find the pergola on fire and bodies hanging from the trees while Mother Courage dragged her cart behind her, selling supplies to the survivors.

To me, a Jew who came to faith late in life, it seems an odd and distant controversy. To me, it seems God works his will in history through the flowering of true ideas while we supply the violence, treachery, and wickedness and so water his garden with our blood. In his book *Inventing the Individual*, philosopher Larry Siedentop describes how the Catholic Church, in staking out its position of power in the aftermath of the classical world, became the vehicle through which the idea of the individual came into being—the individual and his natural right to equal treatment and liberty. But it was only a matter of time before "the egalitarian moral intuitions generated by the church began to be turned against the church itself"[6] as men demanded the freedom to read and interpret Scripture for themselves and to remove the priestly intercessor who made bold to stand between themselves and God.

Before this book is over, I will have to weigh in myself on the mother of God and her sex life, but I'm not here to arbitrate the old grievances. It's God's church, and I believe he intends to unite it again one day if we don't all kill each other first. My only point is that the unfolding of the Reformation argument marks the inevitable coming of unbelief.

~e~

In a way, it's all a question of storytelling. Who gets to define the cultural narrative, and by what authority does he speak? The truth, after all, is a kind of silence—a silent presence, like Jesus at his trial. Things simply are: being, perception, chains of events. It's the stories that we tell about those silent things that give them their shape and meaning: this series of actions and feelings is my self, this piece of earth is my country, these events are my biography, the story of my life. Our stories define what we make of what we experience; they are the lyrics we write to what Seamus Heaney called "the music of what happens."[7]

Who gets to write those lyrics? Who gets to tell those stories? Our churches? Our governments? Each one of us individually? All of us together? Who gets to say what is true about the silent things?

~e~

Take ghosts, for an example very much to the point. What are ghosts anyway? Are they real? What do they tell us about man's fate in the world and beyond the world? So many people have seen ghosts. Often when I'm in a gathering of ten or more, I'll ask if anyone has seen one. There's always someone who has—always: a sane, reasonable person who has had a run-in with a spirit of the dead.

But do we believe them? For the most part, the story we moderns tell about the world doesn't include ghosts. In our modern story, ghosts are illusions, superstitions, misperceptions, dreams. At best they are an outward representation of a psychological fact about the person who perceives them.

But is that what they are really?

Back in Martin Luther's day, it was impossible to dismiss ghosts altogether because there's a ghost mentioned in Scripture, and Scripture was the story that shaped the mind of the time.[8]

The First Book of Samuel tells how King Saul tried to rid Israel of necromancers. It was blasphemy for sorcerers to speak with the dead, so the king began to have them executed. But then the Philistines started to gather a massive army with which to attack Israel. Facing the threat of defeat, the frightened king lost his nerve. He wanted advice from the dead prophet Samuel. So he decided to consult a necromancer himself.

> Saul then said to his attendants, "Find me a woman who is a medium, so I may go and inquire of her."
>
> "There is one in Endor," they said.
>
> So Saul disguised himself, putting on other clothes, and at night he and two men went to the woman. "Consult a spirit for me," he said, "and bring up for me the one I name."
>
> But the woman said to him, "Surely you know what Saul has done. He has cut off the mediums and spiritists from the land. Why have you set a trap for my life to bring about my death?"
>
> Saul swore to her by the LORD, "As surely as the LORD lives, you will not be punished for this."
>
> Then the woman asked, "Whom shall I bring up for you?"
>
> "Bring up Samuel," he said.
>
> When the woman saw Samuel, she cried out at the top of her voice and said to Saul, "Why have you deceived me? You are Saul!"

The king said to her, "Don't be afraid. What do you see?"

The woman said, "I see a ghostly figure coming up out of the earth."

"What does he look like?" he asked.

"An old man wearing a robe is coming up," she said.

Then Saul knew it was Samuel, and he bowed down and prostrated himself with his face to the ground.

Samuel said to Saul, "Why have you disturbed me by bringing me up?"

"I am in great distress," Saul said. "The Philistines are fighting against me, and God has departed from me. He no longer answers me, either by prophets or by dreams. So I have called on you to tell me what to do."

Samuel said, "Why do you consult me, now that the LORD has departed from you and become your enemy? The LORD has done what he predicted through me. The LORD has torn the kingdom out of your hands and given it to one of your neighbors—to David."[9]

And as it was spoken, so it turned out to be. The ghost of the prophet had prophesied the truth.

This biblical scene caused Christian theologians problems from the start. Where had the ghost come from? What did his presence mean about the afterlife? Could the dead rise before judgment day? Did mediums really have the power to speak with them? Some explained it by saying the Witch of Endor was a ventriloquist who tricked Saul by pretending she was Samuel—but that's not in the text. Others said that demons could impersonate the dead—and maybe they can, but that's not in the text either.

And how did they explain all those other ghost sightings—the ghosts people had seen for themselves and the word-of-mouth legends about ghosts and the written accounts of souls who rose from the grave to warn the living to repent of their sins? People had experienced these things. They said they had, anyway. By what story would the church—the final authority on spiritual truth—explain the phenomenon of ghosts?

The doctrine of purgatory gave ghosts a place in the Christian structure of understanding. It made instinctive sense of things. Since most of us are not good enough for heaven as we are, but not really bad enough to spend eternity in hell, why shouldn't there be a punishing half land between damnation and paradise, a zone where our souls can be cleansed of sin until they're fit to enter the presence of God? And whereas the blessed would never leave their bliss, and the cursed could never escape their flaming prison, it seemed reasonable that some of us in-between souls might occasionally rise to give warnings to transgressors. Like the chained and suffering ghost of Jacob Marley in Dickens's *A Christmas Carol*, they would return to offer "a chance and hope of escaping" their fate.[10]

But while the idea of purgatory may have had ancient roots in various funeral practices and prayers for the dead, it too is not in Scripture. It didn't become codified church doctrine until thirteen centuries after the death of Christ. And over the years—though the church did not officially approve of this—the doctrine gave rise to the corrupt practice of selling indulgences. Churchmen would tell believers they could get their loved ones out of purgatory and into heaven faster if they forked over a donation. They even handed out certificates to prove you had bought your dead relatives some centuries of relief.

This—this corruption—is what ticked off Martin Luther in the first place. His famous Ninety-Five Theses was subtitled "Disputation on the Power and Efficacy of Indulgences." Soon, Protestant churches were condemning the idea of purgatory entirely. "It is a fond thing, vainly invented," declared the Protestant Church of England in its founding Thirty-Nine Articles of 1571. "Grounded upon no warranty of Scripture, but rather repugnant to the word of God."[11]

Purgatory was not just a story, in other words, it was a certain kind of story: a false story, a fiction, a lie.

The afterlife, one's fate in the afterlife, the structure of the afterlife, the experience in eternity—these were then, as for many of us they still are, the most important issues of this life, this life we're living. To suddenly discover—or to be forced to confess on pain of death—that your whole idea of eternity was just a tall tale and that the authority on whom you thought your salvation depended was just a tall-tale teller—well, it was like finding out you had to cancel your big trip to Europe because Europe didn't exist; it was just a fantasy your daddy had, a lie your daddy told you, a joke he had played on you.

If you thought about it long enough, deeply enough, it raised the possibility that everything your daddy told you was a lie: everything the church told you, all of church doctrine, and maybe not just the other church's doctrine but your church's doctrine too. Maybe Scripture itself was a lie. Maybe God himself was.

The moment Luther posted his protest in Wittenberg, the chain of thought was inevitable. Since reality was essentially silent, any story anyone told about it might well be just another fiction.

And how could you know reality then? How could you answer Pilate's question, What is truth?

William Shakespeare saw the problem to its depths early on. He understood not only what the Reformation meant but what it was going to mean as the idea of it unfolded in the centuries to come. That, I think, is what the play *Hamlet* is about. As Shakespeare scholar Stephen Greenblatt writes in his book *Hamlet in Purgatory*, it's a story in which "a young man from Wittenberg, with a distinctly Protestant temperament, is haunted by a distinctly Catholic ghost."[12]

A guard cries out as the play begins, "Who's there?"

The guards are nervous outside Elsinore's castle. A ghost has been appearing on the walls. The ghost wants to speak to Prince Hamlet. He says he is the ghost of Hamlet's father, recently dead. And he says he is, indeed, in purgatory:

> Doom'd for a certain term to walk the night
> And for the day confined to fast in fires,
> Till the foul crimes done in my days of nature
> Are burnt and purged away.[13]

It isn't clear when the play takes place, but that doesn't make much difference. It was produced in England around 1600. When the audience heard that Hamlet has been studying in Wittenberg, they had to think of Luther. So, then, when the ghost says he's in purgatory—and when the Church of England says purgatory is "a fond thing . . . repugnant to the Word of God"—Hamlet is in a bind. How can he be sure whether the ghost is "a spirit of health or goblin damn'd," whether he has "intents wicked or charitable"? How can he trust the story the ghost tells him?

And it's quite a story. The ghost of Hamlet's father says he was murdered by his brother Claudius and Hamlet must now avenge his death. Hamlet already hates his uncle because he married his mother so quickly after the king died. So is the ghost telling the truth? Or is he a demon flattering Hamlet's rage?

What is truth? How can he know?

When the play begins, Hamlet is a young man who prides himself on his authenticity, on being what he appears to be. "I know not 'seems,'" he says. The signs of grief he shows for his father—the sighs, the tears, the mourning clothes he wears—these, he says, "are actions that a man might play."[14] But he has that inside himself that "passeth show."

But in his efforts to uncover where the truth lies, he must resort to deception. Like an actor, he must play a part. To hide his suspicions of murder and put Claudius off the trail, he pretends to be mad. But now, his vaunted authenticity is gone. If his inner self and his performance of himself have diverged, how can he know which is real? As he could not tell whether the ghost was speaking truth or not, he cannot now know whether he is actually mad. Maybe he's pretending to be what he really is. How can he decide?

And if he can't know the truth about himself, how can he know the truth about anything? The eye altering alters all. His mood affects his perception of the world. When he's depressed, the "goodly" earth becomes "a sterile promontory," the "majestical" sky becomes "a foul and pestilent congregation of vapors," and humankind, so like the angels, seems to him nothing but the highest order of dust.

As he becomes ever more lost in the maze of philosophical doubt, Hamlet begins to envy those who can play a role with real conviction. If his self is a performance, why can't he feel as deep a belief in it as, say, the actor who can cry while performing the part of Aeneas? Why can't he take action like the soldier willing to die in a fight for a meaningless piece of territory?

By the play's last act, Hamlet has undergone a change. Having faced death at sea, he returns to Denmark with a religious fatalism grounded in gospel wisdom. "There is a divinity that shapes our ends," he says. "There is providence in the fall of a sparrow."[15]

Soon, though, we find him standing in his dead lover's grave, physically fighting with her brother over which of them can appear to grieve more. It's a complete reversal of the play's opening. There, he said his grief surpassed show. Now he brags that he can perform grief better than anyone. He has gone from being what he seems to seeming in order to be. His whole life has become a performance.

At the end of the tragedy, after Hamlet lies dead, his friend Horatio gives the command:

> Bear Hamlet, like a soldier, to the stage;
> For he was likely, had he been put on,
> To have proved most royally.[16]

Hamlet has become *Hamlet*. His life has become the play. He is the story of himself, and the story is all that is left of him.

And so the play begins again with the opening line, "Who's there?"[17]

⟨⟩

What is truth? Who's there? Are we who we think we are, or is our whole life a kind of performance? These aren't just abstract philosophical questions that have no bearing on the way we live. From the moment the Sea of Faith began receding from earth's shore, they were fated to become the questions that would guide and govern and divide and madden and even founder the Christian West. Already, they threaten to transform the civilization that once was Europe—the greatest civilization man has yet made—into a ruin like the forum of Rome.

Without some sort of standard of perception, some kind of received gospel truth, there can be no truth at all that goes unquestioned, no truth we hold self-evident, no axioms of morality, no way to determine what is objectively right and wrong.

From this observation comes the whole dazzling panoply of uncertainty narratives. The Marxist notion of false consciousness: that your general sense of life is a trick played on you by the powerful. You may think you're happy enough working for a living, but it's only because you've accepted the narrative of the evil capitalists who enslave you. The Nietzschean idea that true morality can't be determined. We can do nothing but deconstruct right and wrong until we find its "genealogy," the sources of our fantastical absolutes. The Freudian approach that says your values, your philosophies, even your faith are all projections of animal erotic instincts buried beneath the level of consciousness. Foucault's declaration that all truth systems are merely constructs of the powerful, created to maintain their power. All these philosophies and more are the children of unbelief.

With unbelief, nothing is certain. Nothing is true. Nothing is either good or bad but thinking makes it so—as Hamlet says in his performed madness. Even the meaning of words is suspect, a way the powers that be control your thoughts and actions. They're really just "words, words, words," as mad Hamlet says, not tools for conveying truth, either the truth about the world or the truth about yourself.

Because what is truth? And who's there?

Are you really a woman? Or have you been hoodwinked into femininity by gender social constructs created to keep you in your place? Are you a man or are you "performing masculinity"? Your little boy happily plays with trucks while your daughter prefers dolls, but then they go to school and are taught that they've been deceived into playing roles they do not have to play. They're told they can choose their gender. Is the teacher crazy? Or does she have a point?

Islamist terrorists slaughter thousands of innocents—or are they freedom fighters battling a Western social construct that imprisoned them in the role of the other? A police officer shoots a violent black criminal—or is the cop the criminal and the black man a victim of a system that privileges whiteness so that his criminality is really a kind of justice? Your right to speak your mind, your right to defend yourself by force of arms, your right to profit off hard work and merit, even your right to life—if they are not God given, are they there at all? Or are they illusions of privilege and power designed to hold the underdog in his place?

We sense these uncertainties are deceptions in themselves. They contradict what we know, what we see, what we experience. They even contradict their own logic, because if there is no truth, then how can it be true that there is no truth? And if nothing is good or bad, then why should we seek to fix imbalances of power or any other injustice? But how can we argue the point when they tell us that what we know, what we see, what we experience, even our logic is a construct of false consciousness? How can we stand our ground without seeming—or even being—small minded or intolerant, without spouting idiot bromides like, "Right is right and wrong is wrong!" or, "God said it, I believe it, and that's all there is to it!"

We need God to give us ground to stand on, and not just God, but our God, the Christian God, who will confirm the good values the generations of the West have discerned and learned to live by over time. But we can't just choose belief if we don't, in fact, believe. We need God truly, not just as a useful stopgap against chaos or oppression.

There are those today who call themselves Christian atheists, who want the values of Christianity but can't believe in the religion itself. They say, "Perform faith," or, "Live as if God exists," or, "Let us call ourselves Christians." But they are buying into the premise of uncertainty and deconstructing the very absolute on which they want to depend.

It won't work. It can't work. When we cry out to the universe, "What is truth? Who's there?" we need to be able to hear the voice of some essential reality respond to us: I AM.

⁓

In *Hamlet*, Shakespeare saw that the problem of unbelief was unleashed by the challenge to church authority that had arisen in Wittenberg. But the Enlightenment thinkers who came after him—and those thinkers today who feel the Enlightenment was true to its name—assure us that the problem is no problem at all. We don't need God, they say, not the God of churches and blind faith, anyway. Reason—science—will find the truth, they tell us. Politics will turn that truth into policy. Man alone will make the earth a heaven, or close enough for jazz.

But the Romantics knew better. They were living in the aftermath of the Enlightenment's failure. The Age of Reason had ended with a Reign of Terror. The liberty, fraternity, and equality promised by politics had given way to worldwide war.

So yes, at Haydon's dinner party, on that Immortal Evening, the Romantic poets were there twice. Once in those rooms in the days after the revolution, and once in the painting *Christ's Entry into Jerusalem*. Two of history's spiritual hinges. Two moments when Christ was about to leave the world.

In truth, in both moments, God was already as good as dead in the human heart. The solid ground on which the culture of the West had been built had crumbled. For the Romantics, "It was no longer possible to think, act, write, or paint as if the old forms still had life." Pilate's question was in play again. Hamlet's question. What is truth? Who's there?

CHAPTER 3

UNHALLOWED ARTS

Frankenstein *and the Problem of Science*

No moment of the Immortal Evening was quite so immortal as the poets' toast to Isaac Newton.

Haydon, you'll remember, had painted Newton standing next to Wordsworth watching Christ's entry into Jerusalem. They were there "as believers," Haydon said. Which was fair enough in Newton's case, certainly: his faith may have been eccentric, even heretical, but he was a Christian. The tipsy Lamb wouldn't allow it though. He teased Haydon relentlessly for including in a religious painting the man who invented and symbolized the scientific worldview. Newton, he said, "believed in nothing unless it was as clear as the three sides of a triangle." Keats went along with the joke, wrote Haydon later, saying Newton "had destroyed all the poetry of the rainbow by reducing it to the prismatic colors."

They all drank a toast to "Newton's health, and confusion to mathematics."[1]

~~~

In his book *The Age of Wonder: How the Romantic Generation Discovered the Beauty and Terror of Science*, biographer Richard Holmes says that this moment, this toast, is "thought to exemplify the permanent, instinctive, deep-seated antagonism between Romantic poetry and science."[2] It may even, he says, be the moment from which that canard arose.

But it is a canard—or at least it's simplistic in the extreme. The Romantics didn't hate science at all. Wordsworth, as Holmes points out, had depicted Newton as the ultimate Romantic figure in a poem describing the marble statue of the scientist that stood in the antechapel of Trinity College, Cambridge, where Wordsworth's younger brother, Christopher, was a clergyman and fellow. Wordsworth described the statue's "silent face" as "The marble index of a Mind for ever / Voyaging through strange seas of Thought, alone."[3]

A lone voyager in strange seas is about as Romantic as Romanticism gets.

As for Keats, he had trained as a surgeon and apothecary. He knew how to mix medicines. He had dissected the bodies procured for doctors by the grave robbers known as "resurrection men." He had once described his excitement on reading a powerful translation of Homer by saying it made him feel

> . . . like a watcher of the skies
> When a new planet swims into his ken;
> Or like stout Cortez when with eagle eyes

> He stared at the Pacific—and all his men
> Look'd at each other with a wild surmise.[4]

And all right, it was stout Balboa who discovered the Pacific, but the point remains: Keats was a young man excited by this new epoch of scientific marvels and exploration.

But the wonderful success of science at explaining the material world threatens to create in scientists a bias toward materialism, the idea that there is nothing in life but stuff. What these Romantics feared was not the science itself, and certainly not reason itself, but a growing materialist worldview that threatened to destroy the poetry not of the rainbow but of our experience of the rainbow.

The rainbow, in fact, was the perfect metaphor for the Romantic project. This may be why Wordsworth was moved to write:

> My heart leaps up when I behold
> A rainbow in the sky:
> So was it when my life began;
> So is it now I am a man;
> So be it when I shall grow old,
> Or let me die![5]

As Holmes explains, Newton's experiment with prismatic colors had not destroyed the poetry of the rainbow but, as Keats likely knew, confirmed it: "The point of the experiment was that . . . the rainbow was not a mere scientific trick of the glass prism. It genuinely and beautifully existed in nature, through the natural prism of raindrops, although paradoxically it took a human eye to see it, and every human eye saw it differently."[6] Internal human experience can be creative (the rainbow exists only when I see it), true (I see a rainbow and not a freight train or an oak tree), and unique (I see the rainbow as only I can see it). The Romantics did not want to see Hamlet-like doubts about the nature of reality strip the internal human experience—the spiritual and imaginative life of mankind—of its wholeness, truth, and beauty.

This is what Wordsworth was protesting when he wrote:

> Our meddling intellect
> Misshapes the beauteous forms of things;
> —We murder to dissect.[7]

This was what William Blake was afraid of when he prayed, "May God us keep from Single vision & Newtons sleep."[8]

Think of it this way.

When you see the rain fall, it's not the rain God sees, not the rain as it is, not the fundamental rain. It's the rain man sees: the falling silver rain. But it's true rain, nonetheless. It wets the fields. It makes the crops to grow. Your internal experience is a human version of outer reality.

If a scientist were to say, "I can find the place in your brain where you see the rain. I can touch the place and make you see the rain even when the rain isn't there," and if he then touches that place, you will see the silver rain—you may put your umbrella up, but the crops will die because there is no rain, not really. You would no longer be perceiving what was there. Science would have deluded you out of an internal experience in harmony with the real.

Now, what if you saw—you felt—that you were sad? And what if the scientist said, "I can find the place in your brain where you feel sad. I can touch that place and make you happy instead." And what if he touched the place and you felt happy? Would you be happy, then, in fact? If he touched the place where you feel love, would you be in love?[9]

When I was a young man, I went mad—I wrote about this in my memoir, *The Great Good Thing.* I became delusional and deeply depressed. I was healed by talking to a brilliant psychiatrist. My love for him as a mentor and his genius-level skill at leading me to confront the causes of my madness in childhood traumas brought my mind into harmony with the world as it is. I was then set free to seek what Aristotle called *eudaimonia*, what Christ called life in abundance: a joy centered in physical, moral, and spiritual reality.

But if the same sort of madness afflicted you today, very likely, a shrink would give you drugs.

As I write this, one in ten Americans are being medicated for depression, and yet, as trauma specialist Bessel van der Kolk writes in his book *The Body Keeps the Score,* "it has not made a dent in hospital admissions for depression. The number of people treated for depression has tripled over the past two decades."[10]

Despite that persistent failure, because of scientists' bias toward materialism, it is now the mainstream psychiatric belief that your unhappiness is a chemical event and can therefore be fixed with chemicals. Psychiatrists who still believe in the "talking cure" that healed me are dismissed by their fellow doctors as little more than faith healers. Conversely, those who fully embrace the use of medication are accorded new respect and status because they have joined the medical community's materialist consensus. That, and the cataracts of sweet, sweet money earned by drug companies, provide tremendous incentives to replace treatments that depend on human love, interaction, and understanding with a hot bottle of pills.

None of this is to deny that antidepressants can sometimes be useful tools of treatment, not at all. But I have witnessed myself the results of their reckless overuse. I have heard more than one person say to me, "I feel so much better now," even while I saw the dazed and distant emptiness in their eyes, even when I knew the ghosts that haunted them had not been laid to rest.

When you are drugged out of your sorrows, as a cousin of mine once remarked, "You're still sad, you just can't feel it anymore."

You see the rain, but the crops die.

The success of science in understanding and manipulating nature would ultimately give scientists an aspect of authority even when they spoke on subjects, like religion, they knew nothing about.

Take, for example, lightning.

"For centuries, the devastating scourge of lightning had generally been considered a supernatural phenomenon or expression of God's will. At the approach of a storm, church bells were rung to ward off the bolts. 'The tones of the consecrated metal repel the demon and avert storm and lighting,' declared St. Thomas Aquinas."[11]

So writes Walter Isaacson in his biography of Benjamin Franklin. Franklin noted that the lightning often seemed to respond to the consecrated bells by specifically targeting their church steeples and killing the bell ringers dead. His invention of the lightning rod in 1752, like other inventions and technologies that followed, in no way disproved the possibility of miracles, or the salvation worked in the soul by the death and resurrection of Jesus Christ. But they did create the feeling, the sense, that things just didn't work the way the Bible says they do.

After Franklin, while there were still churches built and they still had steeples, the steeples had lightning rods on top of them. It was a powerful symbol of the new religion that seemed to be replacing the old.

～♥～

Today, as the Romantics feared, we are all materialists in one sense or another. Just listen to how we talk. Instead of saying, "The roller-coaster ride made me excited," we say, "I had an adrenaline rush." Instead of saying, "Running makes me feel great," we say, "Running gives me a dopamine high." We say, "I *have* depression"—I hear this all the time—rather than, "I am depressed." We speak as if our emotions were chemical reactions rather than spiritual reactions communicated to our bodies by chemical means.

～♥～

The summer before the Immortal Evening, the summer of 1816, was a summer of lightning, a summer of storms. A massive volcanic eruption in Indonesia had upended the weather. Temperatures dropped. Crops failed. There was widespread famine. There was rioting in European cities.

In Switzerland that year, on the shore of Lake Geneva, two poets met in May.

George Gordon Byron (Lord Byron) at twenty-eight was already a celebrity, the author of the hugely popular long poem *Childe Harold's Pilgrimage*. It was the story of a brooding, jaded wanderer, weary of sexual escapades—a type that came to be known as the Byronic hero. The poem spoke powerfully to a high British society that had often whiled away the hours of the long war with fashionable promiscuity. Like Harold, they were beginning to feel the "fulness of satiety," and they recognized their own sin-fatigue in Byron's creation. After the publication of the first two cantos in 1812, Byron said, "I awoke one morning and found myself famous."[12]

He was dashing, a nobleman, and debauched—"Mad, bad and dangerous to know," one of his lovers called him.[13] A hot celebrity, he cut a swath through the fine ladies of London—and probably some of the fine gentlemen too. He was finally forced into exile on the continent by the scandal of his collapsing marriage and a rumored affair with his half sister.

The second poet, Percy Bysshe Shelley, was a monied radical, also noble, not a peer but the heir to a baronetcy. He was handsome, high strung, consumptive, and emotionally delicate. He dreamed of a godless world of perfect virtue and free love. He had been expelled from Oxford for publishing atheistic pamphlets and anti-monarchical poetry. That—and his elopement at nineteen with sixteen-year-old Harriet Westbrook—estranged him from his well-to-do father. This made money harder to come by. He had come to Geneva deeply in debt.

Back in England a few years before, Shelley had attached himself to the radical rationalist philosopher William Godwin. Godwin was the widower of another radical, the early feminist Mary Wollstonecraft, the author of *A Vindication of the Rights of Woman*. All of them—Shelley, Godwin, Wollstonecraft—detested the institution of marriage. All of them believed in free love. They had married only for the sake of their children's reputations.

Mary Wollstonecraft had died after giving birth to her

daughter by Godwin, also named Mary. The child was sixteen when the twenty-two-year-old Shelley met her. Whenever he visited Godwin's London home, Shelley would walk with Mary to St. Pancras's churchyard, where Mary's mother was buried. They would sit by her grave, talking about literature and philosophy.

Shelley was still married to Harriet then. They had two children, a baby boy and a one-year-old girl. But free love is free love. Shelley and Mary had soon fallen for one another. They ran away from England together and wandered—romantically, but miserably—across a European continent wracked and ruined by war.

~⁓

By the summer of 1816, Mary was almost nineteen years old. She called herself Mary Shelley now, but she wasn't really. Shelley was still legally married to Harriet, who remained back in England. Mary had given birth to a daughter by Shelley, a premature baby who soon died. The death had shattered her. It haunted her. But she had recently given birth again and the couple now had a four-month-old baby boy.

They were traveling with Mary's stepsister, Claire, who was one year younger than Mary. Claire had also fallen in love with Shelley and may have had an affair with him. But in the spirit of free love, she had redirected her passion into an infatuation for the famous Byron. While they were all still in England, she had pestered Byron into an affair. Now the Shelley party had come to Switzerland because Shelley wanted Claire to arrange a meeting with his celebrated contemporary.

Shelley and Byron were introduced to one another by the shores of Lake Geneva. Researching the second half of *Childe Harold*, Byron had just returned from a tour of the Waterloo battleground and the castles on the Rhine. He was worn out from his journeys. He was irritable. And he was sick of his traveling companion, young Dr. John Polidori.

Byron and Shelley hit it off, though. They both liked sailing, and soon they were out on the lake together every day. Byron enjoyed listening to Shelley's life story, a story almost as sexy and sensational as his own. They both took houses by the water. Byron's was a large, majestic manse with a stately portico—the Villa Diodati, where John Milton had once stayed.

When the storms of that stormy year came in over the mountains, they were all forced inside the villa, Byron, Shelley, Polidori, Mary, and sometimes her baby, and sometimes Claire. Byron would read his new cantos to them, and the conversations that followed would go on so long into the night that Shelley and his party would often have to stay over. Claire would make her way to Byron's bedroom. "If a girl of eighteen comes prancing to you at all hours—there is but one way," Byron sighed Byronically.[14]

Mary was a strange creature to be among this crew. Quiet and dreamy where the others were fractious, voluble, and intense, she was, she said later, "a devout but nearly silent listener" to the poets' philosophical debates.[15]

Given her parentage and background, it was natural for her to consider a literary career, but more than writing she enjoyed "the formation of castles in the air—the indulging in waking dreams . . . My dreams were at once more fantastic and agreeable than my writings. In the latter I was a close imitator . . . doing as others had done . . . but my dreams were all my own."[16]

She was smart, pretty, entrancingly feminine, deeply devoted to the powerful men in her life. Her father, she said, had been a god to her, and she made a god of Shelley after him. Under his influence, she mimicked his extreme philosophies, even though she never seemed truly to embrace them deep down. He was an atheist. "I can scarcely set bounds to my hatred of Christianity," he said.[17] But she, while suspicious of organized religion, seemed to share her mother's lifelong faith in a God very much like the Christian God. Shelley was a political radical, but after he was gone, Mary wrote, "I have no wish to ally myself to the Radicals—they are full of repulsion to me—violent without any sense of Justice—selfish in the extreme—talking without knowledge—rude, envious and insolent."[18] He sometimes encouraged her to have love affairs as he did, and sometimes she may have gone along, but it was always him she wanted. The great poet died young, but she adored him all her life.

Like Wordsworth, Mary grew more conservative as she grew older. Like him, she fit well into the Victorian age that followed. She became more conventionally religious too. She seemed to adopt many of the ideas of the traditionalist Evangelicals who had helped transform the promiscuous high society of the Regency into Victorian moralists. Her later writings emphasize the Evangelical ideal of women as the silent saints of domestic life, whose pious qualities, described in one publication of the time, were "submission, love, tenderness, self-sacrifice, devotement, sympathy."[19]

I don't think this was just the influence of Victorian religious philosophy, though. These qualities already seemed to be latent in her, even among radicals, even in that summer of lightning, 1816.

One night that summer, as the party sheltered in the villa from the bad weather, the poets began to read ghost stories from a book called *Fantasmagoriana*. It was a German collection originally, but they read it in a French translation. The ghosts in these stories were spirits damned by their sins to punish others for their sins. One story called "The Death-Bride," for instance, told of the phantom of an unfaithful woman who animates the bodies of dead women in order to seduce and murder unfaithful men.

After they'd been reading a while, Lord Byron declared to the group, "We will each write a ghost story."[20] This, anyway, is how Mary remembered it.

Over the next days, Byron and Shelley each began to write a ghostly tale, but both tales trailed off. They were never finished. Polidori eventually reworked Byron's story into his sexually charged novella *The Vampyre*. It was the first full-length vampire story. Published a few years later, it became an enormous success. It's still an enjoyable read today.

As for Mary: "I busied myself *to think of a story*—a story to rival those which had excited us to this task. One which would speak to the mysterious fears of our nature, and awaken thrilling horror— one to make the reader dread to look round, to curdle the blood, and quicken the beatings of the heart."

Days went past and inspiration wouldn't come to her. "*Have you thought of a story?* I was asked each morning, and each morning I was forced to reply with a mortifying negative."[21]

Then one night, as lightning came flashing in over the lake-water, the conversation in the villa turned to the subject of electricity. Shelley had always been interested in this. In his college days at Oxford, he had filled his room with electrical devices. His friend T. J. Hogg would help attach the wires to him and then shock him until "his long, wild locks bristled and stood on end."[22]

Mary, meanwhile, had recently been reading about the experiments of an Italian physician, Giovanni Aldini—the nephew of Luigi Galvani, from whom galvanism took its name. In a public exhibition, Aldini had pumped electricity into the corpse of an executed criminal. The charges caused the body to twitch enough "almost to give an appearance of re-animation."[23]

The idea of reanimation had haunted Mary's dreams as well.[24] The year before, in the mournful days after her first child died, she had written in her journal about a dream in which she and Shelley had laid the infant before a fire and rubbed it until "my little baby came to life again."[25]

Now, as the storm went on outside, she listened as the poets discussed "various philosophical doctrines . . . among others the nature of the principle of life, and whether there was any probability of its ever being discovered and communicated."

When the conversation ended, Mary went to bed. As she lay there awake, her eyes closed, one of her daydreams unfolded before her.

"My imagination, unbidden, possessed and guided me, gifting the successive images that arose in my mind with a vividness far beyond the usual bounds of reverie. I saw—with shut eyes, but acute mental vision—I saw the pale student of unhallowed arts kneeling beside the thing he had put together. I saw the hideous phantasm of a man stretched out, and then, on the working of some powerful engine, show signs of life, and stir with an uneasy, half vital motion."[26]

At last, she had her story. This was the inspiration for her first novel: *Frankenstein*.

~ co

Frankenstein was not a success when it was first published two years later.[27] It sold fewer than five hundred copies and then vanished into obscurity. But after only a few years, sensational theatrical versions of the story began to appear. These stage plays were made without Mary's permission and she wasn't paid for them, but she enjoyed them nonetheless. "In the early performances, all the ladies fainted and hubbub ensued!" she reported happily.[28] It was the plays that made her—and her monster—famous.

These productions weren't much like the novel though. Mary had created Victor Frankenstein as a complex and tormented thinker, his better nature struggling against his dark ideas. The creature he creates is a brooding, yearning, eloquent, and all-too-human criminal. It is the anguish of loneliness and rejection that pushes him to murderous rage.

In the plays, on the other hand, Frankenstein is a mad scientist bent over buzzing, flashing, lightning-like equipment with his comical humpbacked assistant—Fritz or Igor—gibbering by his side. This version of the story was the inspiration for the Universal Studios movie series in the 1930s.

~ co

The second movie in that series, *Bride of Frankenstein*, is a great film, but it begins with a wonderfully bad reenactment of the famous Diodati gathering where the story was first conceived.

Here, the villa is transformed into a crumbling gothic castle—but only on the outside. Inside, weirdly, there's a comfortable and civilized Regency drawing room so enormous that a parlor maid can take three Irish wolfhounds for a walk across the floor. Lord Byron, Shelley, and Mary are gathered there by a gigantic fireplace. Violin parlor music is playing—somehow. And lightning flashes at the windows.

Byron, rolling his *r*'s like bowling balls down a long lane, declares that the storm outside may be Jehovah's expression of rage against him because he is "England's grrrrreatest sinner." That's actually something Byron almost might have said, but the idea that he would then also declare Shelley, rather than himself, "England's grrreatest poet," is more unbelievable than anything else in the movie, or in any movie.

But the point of the scene is delivered by a dainty, coy, and yet mystically all-knowing Mary, played by the incomparable English actress Elsa Lanchester. With a pretty girlish giggle, she reassures the audience that the horror flick they're about to see contains "a moral lesson. The punishment that befell a mortal man who dared to emulate God!"[29]

The real-life Mary also hinted at this moral in her famous introduction to the novel's 1831 republication. "Supremely frightful would be the effect of any human endeavor to mock the stupendous mechanism of the Creator of the world," she wrote.[30]

But I don't think this is what the novel is about at all. What fascinates me about the story, anyway—what makes it great both for itself and as the source material for all the many works it has inspired over more than two centuries—is not that Victor Frankenstein usurps the rights of God. After all, in fashioning a new creature out of corpses, he does no more than what men have always done: he makes new life out of existing materials.

To me, the greatness of the story, the horror of the story, and the threat to humanity the story portrays lie in the fact that

Frankenstein has usurped the power not of God but of women. He has made a man without a mother. His science has eliminated the principle of femininity from the creation of human life.

In his epic of self-examination, *The Prelude, or Growth of a Poet's Mind*, William Wordsworth speculates that the internal human experience is galvanized into existence by our first interchanges with our mothers. It's a remarkable, even groundbreaking, passage of profound insight:

> Blest the infant Babe . . .
> Nursed in his Mother's arms, who sinks to sleep
> Rocked on his Mother's breast; who with his soul
> Drinks in the feelings of his Mother's eye!
> For him, in one dear Presence, there exists
> A virtue which irradiates and exalts
> Objects through widest intercourse of sense.
> No outcast he, bewildered and depressed:
> Along his infant veins are interfused
> The gravitation and the filial bond
> Of nature that connect him with the world.[31]

The experience of his mother's love allows the new soul to become a self. All nature around him becomes infused and alive with his mother's love so that he feels connected to the world and sympathizes with its afflictions and pains. He becomes

> An inmate of this active universe:
> For, feeling has to him imparted power

That through the growing faculties of sense
Doth like an agent of the one great Mind
Create, creator and receiver both,
Working but in alliance with the works
Which it beholds. —Such, verily is the first
Poetic spirit of our human life.[32]

Through mother love, humans learn to become "agents of the one great Mind." Each of us begins to fashion a distinct and unique experience of the living world, a new creation made in collaboration with God out of our engagement with his creation, which is nature.

As it turns out, Wordsworth's brilliant spiritual insight has a physical analogue as well. Researchers have now discovered what are called mirror neurons in the cortex of the brain. According to Dr. Van der Kolk these neurons explain "many previously unexplainable aspects of the mind, such as empathy, imitation, synchrony, and even the development of language."[33]

These neurons seem to become active as soon as babies are born—maybe even before that, in the womb. In the child's first interactions with its mother, the two enter what Van der Kolk calls a "dance of attunement."[34] Through these mirror neurons, mother and child's "physical interactions lay the groundwork for baby's sense of self—and, with that, a lifelong sense of identity."[35]

It is in the physical world just as Wordsworth described it spiritually: the child drinks creative individuality from his mother's eyes.

The unique power of the feminine, then, is not just to confer life on matter but to infuse life with creative humanity. Even God, when he wanted to become human, chose for himself a mother. Without the experience of the feminine, a person may well become, as Wordsworth says, an "outcast . . . bewildered and depressed."

This is exactly what happens to Frankenstein's motherless monster.

～ल

Perhaps subconsciously, Mary Shelley seems to have noted that a tension was growing up between science, with its materialist bias, and women, the conduit for the spiritual life of mankind. Already, in Mary's time, science and the technology it created had severely disrupted women's lives.

Consider the picture of a preindustrial woman in an oft-quoted chapter of the Bible, Proverbs 31. This is the chapter that includes the question, "Who can find a virtuous woman, for her price is far above rubies?" The chapter goes on to describe such a woman, and it's easy to see what drove her price up so high. She is not only a font of wisdom, goodness, and charity, she is a powerful economic engine as well. She makes clothes and linens for her own family, and then sells the excess at market for a profit. She barters for property and buys it, and then uses her earnings to plant a vineyard on it. And all the while, she rises "while it is yet night" to make sure everyone in her household is fed. No wonder rubies don't begin to cover her worth.

But with the coming of the Industrial Revolution in the mid-eighteenth century, much of the practical and economic usefulness of women began to be stripped away. Factories destroyed many of the home industries that gave women their rubies-plus economic standing. Women were once called the "distaff," after the device with which they made clothing—a hugely important enterprise, almost as necessary as food, which women also helped create. Now, with the new machines, cheap, inexpensive clothing was made in "dark, Satanic mills" outside the home. Food, utensils, furniture would all one day be mass produced. Men, without babies at their breasts, could leave their farmland for the cities to work in the new mills, but over time, to become a wife, a mother, a homemaker, meant to "leave the workforce" and become an economic "dependent," rather than a central part of an in-house economic system of mutual sustenance and wealth creation.

Even the unmitigated blessing—the incalculable blessing—of better health care that drastically reduced the deaths of children—medical science's greatest glory—also, in a strange sense, reduced the value of women as the living factories of humankind. It now required less production to meet the quota, as it were. And those children women did produce were less economically valuable than they had been. Children were once called "the poor man's riches," because they helped work the land, continued the family business and cared for and supported parents in their old age. Now factories called these children away to the cities from which, often, they never returned. Today, unless you happen to have a child, probably a daughter, who takes care of you in your dotage, children are entirely an economic outlay.

The Victorians tried to compensate women for the diminishment of their material usefulness by hyperemphasizing their spiritual roles as wives, mothers, and homemakers, as in this popular verse by William Ross Wallace:

> Woman, how divine your mission
> Here upon our natal sod!
> Keep, oh, keep the young heart open
> Always to the breath of God!
> All true trophies of the ages

Are from mother-love impearled;

For the hand that rocks the cradle

Is the hand that rules the world.[36]

The mom-sage-creator-businesswoman-homemaker of Proverbs 31 became the *Angel in the House*, a sentimental picture that hung in many Victorian homes inspired by a hugely popular and absolutely dreadful poem of the same name by Coventry Patmore:

Her beauty was a godly grace;

The mystery of loveliness,

Which made an altar of her face,

Was not of the flesh, though that was fair,

But a most pure and living light

Without a name, by which the rare

And virtuous spirit flamed to sight.[37]

Women may be forgiven for not wanting to have their faces used for altars and, in general, for desiring to live out their lives on earth as something more substantial than a comforting ethereal presence flickering about the living room like Tinker Bell in a stage production of *Peter Pan*. Because the fact is, with the possible exception of my wife, women are not angels. Their spiritual femininity is made manifest in female people who can reasonably be expected to desire an acknowledged value in the society they inhabit.

Always and everywhere throughout history, women's scope of action has been restricted, but their role, their purpose, their value to society was crystal clear. Now, with that role diminished, the restrictions began to become intolerable. I don't think it's a coincidence that protofeminists like Mary Wollstonecraft came into being at exactly the same time as the Industrial Revolution. It is the moment when women's essential economic contributions began to be undermined, and the integrated social role of spiritual femininity was sundered from women's physical existence.

~❧

The march of technology also brought materialism in its wake like a camp-following prostitute, and that had its effect on women too. What is "free love," after all, but materialism in the flesh?

The church had spent centuries trying to spiritualize eros, morally binding sexuality to its procreative function, transforming marriage into a sacrament that demanded fidelity from husbands as well as wives, inventing the ideals of chivalry that put men's warrior strength at the service of the chaste feminine. All this tended to elevate women to equal humanity with men—philosophically at least. But with religion beginning its long death spin, the avant-garde foresaw a better way: forget all that church stuff and have lots of sex.

Mary Wollstonecraft had protested against the sexual double standard that prized chastity in women but despised it in men. All well and good, but the practical penalties of sexual freedom did not fall on the two sexes equally.

The wife that Percy Shelley had left behind when he eloped with Mary was devastated by her abandonment. A few months after Mary first conceived *Frankenstein*, Harriet drowned herself in the Serpentine in London's Hyde Park, orphaning her two children by Shelley, and killing the baby of another man that was then inside her.

Much as she loved her father and Shelley, Mary also suffered from their radical new morality. When the baby she had been nursing in the summer of lightning died two years later, her father was brutally cold about what she called her "wretchedness and despair." He scolded her in exasperation, mocking her because "all the rest of the world . . . is nothing because a child of two years old is dead."[38]

Shelley saw her maternal grief entirely as an inconvenience to himself. He wrote in his notebook:

> My dearest Mary, wherefore hast thou gone,
> And left me in this dreary world alone?
> Thy form is here indeed—a lovely one—
> But thou art fled, gone down a dreary road
> That leads to Sorrow's most obscure abode.
> For thine own sake I cannot follow thee
> Do thou return for mine.[39]

He entertained himself during her fits of depression with idealized dalliances with other women.

As for Claire, her renewed affair with Byron produced a child, Alba. But by then, the poet was bored with Claire's emotionalism and cast her off. When she couldn't afford to raise the little girl, Byron took charge of her but at a steep price. He imperiously renamed the girl Allegra, and all but banned the brokenhearted Claire from the little girl's life. He then placed the child in a Catholic convent. She died there of typhus at the age of five.

Future generations would solve the material inequalities in the sex lives of men and women by means of birth control and abortion. Through the miracle of science, a woman can now medicate her body so that men may use it for their pleasure without consequence or attachment. And, should the medication fail, she is free to have doctors kill the child in her womb and drag it out in pieces to be sold for profit and used for medical experimentation.

It seems possible to me that a spiritually whole woman might regard this system as an endless nightmare of abuse, a cancellation of her feminine humanity in service to the libertine pleasures of soul-dead men. Perhaps such women will one day reject the system outright. Perhaps they will begin to turn technology to their own purposes and use it to reestablish the sort of home industries that will allow them to live a modern life more like the life of Proverbs 31.

Or perhaps, in accepting the world as purely material, women will teach themselves to feel that promiscuity and abortion are what freedom and equality look like. Time will tell.

In any case, in later years, the embittered Claire wrote this: "The worshippers of free love not only preyed upon one another, but preyed equally upon their own individual selves turning their existence into a perfect hell . . . Under the influence of the doctrine and belief of free love I saw the two first poets of England . . . become monsters of lying, meanness, cruelty and treachery."[40]

A great writer writing herself writes her time, and in writing her time she writes the future. By 1816, there was already evidence that science, technology, and the materialism that comes with them could one day make women extraneous and turn men into monsters. What Mary Shelley did was simply imagine that trend into its worst-case scenario.

In doing so, she invented the science-fiction novel.

Frankenstein begins in the Arctic. Captain Robert Walton, guiding his ship through polar ice, rescues a dying man from the water: Victor Frankenstein. Frankenstein is a lone voyager in strange seas. He is hunting across the floes the monster he created. He tells the captain his story.

He speaks of his mother, a near perfect model of feminine virtues—loving, devoted, patient in adversity, the whole lot. Victor's Genovese childhood is idyllic, shared with the family's adopted daughter, Elizabeth. Elizabeth, he says, is his "more than sister—the beautiful and adored companion of all my occupations and my pleasures."[41] They are tacitly engaged to marry.

When his mother dies of scarlet fever in his seventeenth year, Victor leaves home and begins his scientific studies at the University of Ingolstadt in Germany. Sunk in grief, he is drawn into dark arts. He conceives his great and terrible idea.

Obsessed with creating a human being, he builds a creature out of body parts. He uses electricity to galvanize it into life. But when the thing awakes, he too awakes from his fixation. He suddenly finds himself horrified by the creature he has made.

He escapes to his room. He falls into a troubled sleep and is "disturbed by the wildest dreams."

"I thought I saw Elizabeth, in the bloom of health, walking in the streets of Ingolstadt. Delighted and surprised, I embraced her, but as I imprinted the first kiss on her lips, they became livid with the hue of death; her features appeared to change, and I thought that I held the corpse of my dead mother in my arms; a shroud enveloped her form, and I saw the grave-worms crawling in the folds of the flannel."[42]

This dream—this appalling dream—spells out the horror of what he's done. It is inspired, I think, by the story *The Death Bride* from *Fantasmagoriana*, which Mary later misremembered as "the History of the Inconstant Lover, who, when he thought to clasp the bride to whom he had pledged his vows, found himself in the arms of the pale ghost of her whom he had deserted."[43]

Here, Victor runs into the arms of the woman he hopes to marry, presumably the mother of his future children. They kiss— and as they kiss, she morphs into his dead mother, rotten in her grave. Life becomes death, creation becomes murder. In making a man without a woman, he has usurped Elizabeth's purpose and power and so transformed her into the dead, rotten ruin of a mother.

Meanwhile, the creature he made, despised, persecuted, and alone, hides out near a happy emigre family. By observing and eavesdropping on them, he educates himself about the ways of humankind: "I heard of the difference of sexes, and the birth and growth of children, how the father doted on the smiles of the infant, and the lively sallies of the older child, how all the life and cares of the mother were wrapped up in the precious charge, how the mind of youth expanded and gained knowledge, of brother, sister, and all the various relationships which bind one human being to another in mutual bonds."[44]

By the time his creator tracks him to his hiding place, the monster knows exactly what he needs in order to become fully human. He demands that Frankenstein complete his creative work and make for him an Eve.

Frankenstein begins the dreadful business, but he can't bring himself to finish it. He destroys the man-made woman before she is done. Enraged, the monster cries out, "I, too, can create desolation!"[45] Again and again, he threatens him: "I will be with you on your wedding night."[46]

He is. He murders Elizabeth. He turns Frankenstein's dream into a horrible reality: The future mother of his children becomes a corpse. He is left alone with no purpose in life but to hunt his creature down and kill it.

─ℯ

As generations passed, the genre Mary Shelley launched—science fiction—moved steadily to the center of popular entertainment. I watched this happen.

When I was growing up, there were no home methods of recording movies. The only films I could watch outside of the theater were those that were played late at night on TV: old movies, the same movies my parents saw when they were growing up. The genres I was drawn to were mostly crime stories, westerns, war stories, and the occasional soap opera: genres about the present and the past. For me, they were a way of learning the old values. The West was settled and the war was over and likely I'd never have to solve a crime, but surely the future would not look too different from what had gone before. The values and talents that solved problems in my father's day would still come in handy for me.

I loved monster movies too. But these were also about the present and the past. Their vampires, werewolves, mummies, and creatures from the Black Lagoon were human-sized beasts, often remnants of ancient civilizations or the products of ancient curses. In attempting to carry off the scantily clad, eek-screaming heroines, they represented the unbridled masculine aggression that a boy had to learn to control in order to make his world safe for order, domesticity, and love. The movies taught chivalry, in other words.

Even the most popular science fiction then was largely inspired by history. The TV show *Star Trek*—a reinvention of C. S. Forester's Hornblower novels about the Napoleonic War at sea—projected the old imperial narratives into deep space. *Star Wars* took place "a long time ago" and fused ancient mythology with knightly values as well as moral conflicts drawn from the American Revolution.

I did read Marvel and DC comic books with their fantastic futuristic stories about men and women with superpowers. I read them right up until I reached the age of twelve or so. Somehow, when I discovered girls, these vaguely sexless superheroes struck me as childish and silly.

But it is not so with young men today. The supermen and superwomen of those comics dominate the entertainment industry now. Men well into their thirties and forties discuss the films arising from the Marvel and DC "universes" with intensity and passion. Critics see social importance in them. Viewers who did not go into ecstasies over a wooden piece of second-rate silliness like *Black Panther* were suspected of being racist because the hero was black. Women—grown women, I mean, with college educations—shed tears during the film *Wonder Woman* when the superheroine stormed the German trenches in World War I because . . . well, I don't know why. I guess because, at long last, a female who never existed had won a battle that never happened in a manner completely unlike anything that could ever occur in real life.

The superpeople depicted in these comic-book films might get killed (until they are resurrected for a sequel), but they are not inherently mortal. They do not grow old as we who are not super grow old. Many of them wear skintight outfits that emphasize their male muscularity or female shapeliness. But their costumes are often seamless, with no easy way in or out, symbolic of the heroes' essential sexlessness. By virtue of their strength, the super-women are (depending on how you look at it) either liberated from or deprived of the natural vulnerabilities and processes that being a woman normally entails. The men are therefore absolved of their chivalrous responsibilities to protect and support them and their children.

All of which is to say these films don't deal with the problems of *eros* and *thanatos*—the problems of being a sexual and therefore finite creature—which is also to say they do not deal with the experience of being human as we have known it for all the centuries that have gone before.

With the quickening advance of technology, the mind of the culture has turned from learning the values of the past to imagining an utterly transformed human enterprise. Superhero stories are, I think, prophecies of a coming transhuman world. They foresee a time when machines can be implanted in our bodies to make us smarter, stronger, faster, perhaps even immortal—supermen and superwomen.

I watched films that prepared me for a future like the past. Today's young people are watching films that prepare them for a future like no past has ever been.

—e·o—

Perhaps this effectively genderless and possibly deathless trans-human future will actually solve the problems of *eros* and *thanatos*. Perhaps we will shed the anxieties and glories of our old-fashioned humanity like a dead skin. The humanizing influences of femininity will become unnecessary, obsolete. Our spiritual elevation of motherhood will seem a romantic relic. Tomorrow's women may roll their eyes at the thought that their foremothers had to endure nine months of discomfort and inconvenience to do what is now done by an oversized toasterlike gizmo in the kitchen. Or perhaps so-called sex-change operations will no longer be a cosmetic illusion reenforced by the misuse of him and her pronouns, but a genuine fact of technological life. Perhaps then the humanizing tasks of femininity—creating life out of matter, homes out of houses, minds out of brains, and souls out of bodies—will fall equally on the genders or will be chosen like a profession by anyone who happens to have the talent and proclivity. Perhaps the passions and fears of our mortal, gendered life—the passions and fears that now define us whether it is politically correct to admit it or not—will be seen to have been a mere inconvenience of a prior age of ignorance and primitivism.

Or perhaps, by losing those passions and fears, by losing our genders and our mortality, we will have lost our essential selves. Perhaps in eradicating our troubles we will have created nothing but a convenient little nightmare of purely materialist existence, a depersonalized personhood in a world less fit for man than for machines.

$$\sim$$

It is interesting to me that in the late 1960s and '70s—the period of transition from a tradition-based culture to a technology-expectant culture—almost all the most important, iconic, and successful horror movies were based on a fear of female biological processes. The blockbuster *The Exorcist* (1973) essentially reimagined a young girl's menarche as a tale of demonic possession. *Carrie* (1976) begins with a girl experiencing her first period and ends with her bathed in blood after she has used her newfound telekinetic powers to destroy everyone around her. In *Rosemary's Baby* (1968) and *The Omen* (1976), the devil takes a hand in the process of childbirth, impregnating one poor lady directly and giving a satanic changeling to another. And in *Alien* (1979), a female beast plants her embryos in men who then explode in a monstrous parody of birth. A woman must take on the male hero role to restore order.

These films reflect a growing estrangement from the natural feminine, and therefore from the human. They contain within them a fearful premonition of a genderless future of human objects, more *its* than *he's* and *she's*. Their era is bookended by *Psycho* in 1960 and *The Silence of the Lambs* in 1991, both horrific depictions of murderous transgenderism inspired by the real-life killer Ed Gein. Gein killed women and dressed in their skins in order to feel closer to his mother.

It was very much as if our collective unconscious had finally caught on to what Mary Shelley was brooding over more than two centuries before: the only thing standing between us and our perfect but soulless materialist destiny is the inconvenient fertility of the female body and the humanity-producing power of motherly love.

⁓

In the nightmare version of our daydreamed future, the machines we originally made to serve us entirely replace us and make us their slaves. In the 1984 sci-fi film *The Terminator*, these ruling machines must suppress a human rebellion. So what do they do? They send an android hitman back in time to kill the woman who will become the mother of the rebel leader.

What is so brilliant about this near-perfect little action movie is that the mother, Sarah Connor, is not special or heroic at all. She's "just a girl." That's her superpower. Her very girliness—her femininity—is in itself the central threat to the machine empire. In the *Terminator* sequels, of course, Sarah is transformed into a muscular faux male action hero, suitable for feminist viewing. Which suggests that perhaps these future machine tyrants have already won the day by winning over our minds so that we cannot picture femininity as a power in itself.

It is little wonder that the ultimate movie vision of machines ruling over mankind was created by two transgender people, once the Wachowski Brothers, now known as the Wachowski Sisters. The machine-made universe in their movie series is called *The Matrix*, a word that descends from the Latin word for womb. But it's the machines that have seized the feminine power of creation now so that the creation is therefore mechanical and fake. The Matrix is a make-believe human existence, a machine-created illusion, by which humanity is stupefied into passivity so that our brains can be used as batteries to power the triumphant machines. People have transformative powers of mind in the Matrix, but only because they are not living in the real human world.

They see the spiritual rain, but the soul, unwatered, dies.

Materialism is, of course, by nature hostile toward spiritual humanity. That hostility plays itself out in the inherent tension between technology and the human feminine—the feminine, which brings life into matter and spiritual being into life. The threat that technology will render womanhood obsolete is, I believe, the unconscious fear that powers the more antifeminine strains of feminism: those strains that can imagine women's "empowerment" only in traditionally male terms of physical strength, career success, and work in scientific professions centered on things rather than the professions centered on people that women all over the world prefer. The antifeminine cohort recoil at such Mary-Shelleyan qualities as "submission, love, tenderness, self-sacrifice, devotement, sympathy." They even wish to eliminate femininity entirely by declaring gender a mere social construct which is therefore infinitely mutable and specific to no one sex. They are hiding from the Terminator by allying themselves with the materialism of the machines they fear will one day rule.

But the threat is to both sexes really. The threat is that the blessings of science could blind us to its materialist curse, and that in triumphing over the problems of *eros* and *thanatos* that arise from being gendered creatures, science might one day triumph over humanity itself.

This threat is what Mary Shelley portrayed in her wonderful, genre-creating work. Girlish Mary, devoted Mary, mother Mary, still mourning the death of one child while nursing another, sitting as "a devout but nearly silent listener," while Byron and Shelley, moonstruck by their own desires, bloviated brilliantly on the possibility of making life through lightning, life without the intrusion of the feminine, life without the likes of Mary Shelley.

Well, she gave them their lightning, all right. It is featured in one of the most terrific passages in gothic literature, in any literature.

As Victor Frankenstein is returning home to Switzerland in the dark of night, lightning suddenly strikes and reveals his monster standing right before him. There in the white gleam of the power that first animated him is the murderer of "all the various relationships which bind one human being to another in mutual bonds."[47]

"A flash of lightning illuminated the object, and discovered its shape plainly to me; its gigantic stature, and the deformity of its aspect, more hideous than belongs to humanity, instantly informed me that it was the wretch, the filthy daemon, to whom I had given life . . . The figure passed me quickly, and I lost it in the gloom . . . I thought of pursuing the devil; but it would have been in vain, for another flash discovered him to me hanging among the rocks of the nearly perpendicular ascent of Mont Saleve . . . He soon reached the summit, and disappeared."[48]

In this worst of worst-case scenarios, the wifeless creator and the motherless creature end up pursuing each other across the ice of a vast, sterile Arctic landscape, a landscape from which every trace of femininity—and therefore of humanity—is gone at last.

CHAPTER 4

TO REIGN IN HELL

Paradise Lost *and the*
Problem of Radical Politics

Both evenings were haunted by the loss of paradise, the fall of man. At both the lightning-struck gathering of radicals by Lake Geneva in 1816, and the hilarious hey-diddle drink-fest of the more conservative Romantics in London the next year, the expulsion from the garden of Eden was woven like an undertheme into the conversations.

We know it was on Mary Shelley's mind. Her novel is laced with meditations on and references to *Paradise Lost*, John Milton's seventeenth-century poetic masterpiece dramatizing Satan's rebellion and Adam's fall. She used a quote from it as her epigraph for *Frankenstein*; Adam's anguished cry to God on being cast out of Eden becomes the monster's cry to his creator: "Did I request thee, Maker, from my clay to mould me man? Did I solicit thee from darkness to promote me?"[1]

Wordsworth was thinking of Milton too. In later years, looking back fondly on the Immortal Evening, Benjamin Haydon remembered Wordsworth's "fine intonation" as he quoted the poet to the other dinner guests. But then, Wordsworth was almost always thinking of Milton. He was haunted by him, driven by him, led by him and by *Paradise Lost*. He believed himself to be Milton's successor in English poetical greatness. He spent—and possibly wasted—a great deal of his creative energies trying to conceive of and create an epic that would compete with his.

All of them—all the Romantics—had this in common with Milton. They had lived through a king-killing revolution that had succeeded, and then utterly failed. In recreating Satan's rebellion and Adam's disobedience, Milton was struggling to come to terms with his own rebellion and disobedience during the English Civil War and the execution of Charles I. And now—in the aftermath of Waterloo—Mary, Shelley, Wordsworth, Keats—all of them—were trying to come to terms with the collapse of the French Revolution, a rebellion that had been supposed to issue in a new political paradise and had instead transformed the European continent into an inferno of terror and war.

"Bliss was it in that dawn to be alive, but to be young was very heaven!"[2] That was how Wordsworth remembered the outbreak of the revolution in *The Prelude*. He was a young man—nineteen—when the fighting started. Like many of his contemporaries, he was idealistic enough to believe that now "the meagre, stale, forbidding ways of custom, law and statute" would be overthrown in the name of a new and glorious Age of Reason.[3]

He was an aimless student at Cambridge then, uncertain of what he wanted to do with his life. The next year, when he was twenty, in the summer of 1790, he traveled to France to begin an alpine hiking tour. Like any writer—any artist—he wanted to see for himself what was happening. But he wasn't really all that interested in the politics of it:

> A stripling, scarcely of the household then
> Of social life, I looked upon these things
> As from a distance.[4]

He arrived in Calais just in time for the one-year-anniversary celebration of the storming of the Bastille. This was supposed to mark the revolution's successful conclusion: the overthrow of the ancient regime, the beginning of a constitutional monarchy. The citizens were jubilant. Looking at them, Wordsworth saw "How bright a face is worn when joy of one is joy for tens of millions."[5]

But that was enough of that. He was in a hurry to get on with his walking tour of the Alps.

He returned to France the next year, though. That's when the spirit of radicalism really caught hold of him. He was still a lost youth at this point. He was drifting toward a life in the priesthood, but without much in the way of conviction or passion. Travel was, in part, a way of delaying the day of decision.

He made his way to Orleans. There, he met a fiercely intelligent twenty-five-year-old woman named Annette Vallon. She gave him French lessons—in every sense of the term, apparently, since she was soon pregnant by him.

Annette was Catholic, likely a royalist. But when the lovestruck Wordsworth trailed after her to her hometown of Blois, he met and befriended a revolutionary nobleman there. The cavalry captain Michel de Beaupuy was fifteen years Wordsworth's senior, a romantic figure who had a way with women. He became William's political mentor.

As his affair with Annette continued hot, Wordsworth would walk and talk with Beaupuy beside the blue waters of the broad river Loire and on into the woods outside the city. Under Beaupuy's tutelage, Wordsworth wrote, "hatred of absolute rule, where will of one is law for all . . . laid stronger hold daily upon me." Once, when the two of them passed by a "hunger-bitten" girl straggling along beside her "languid" cow as it searched the lane for food, Beaupuy pointed at her and said, "'Tis against *that* which we are fighting."[6]

This kind of rhetoric made stirring lyrics to go with the music of his first passionate love affair. Soon, Wordsworth was all het up with revolutionary fervor. His personal history probably fed his political feelings too. When he was young, after his father died, a local aristocrat had ruined his family by refusing to pay his debts to them. Wordsworth had good reason to sympathize with an uprising by the lowly against the upper classes.

Unfortunately, he had the political timing of a poet. Just as he signed on for *liberte*, *egalite*, and *fraternite*, the whole enterprise started to go very badly wrong.

Robespierre and the radical, bloodthirsty Jacobins were on the rise. No longer was the revolution a means of merely reforming the old government. Now France was to be fundamentally transformed into a crystal city of immaculate goodness, justice falling on the thirsty multitudes like rain. Every inequality would vanish. The past would be reviled and the statues of the old heroes would be torn down. The very names of the months would change, and the new republican calendar would be freed from any reference to gods or kings. Religion would fall. Reason would rule. And of course anyone who wasn't willing to be reasonable would be reasonably slaughtered.

With the logic of all political utopians, murder began to seem to the Jacobins a tool of virtue. The only thing standing in the way of human perfection, after all, is humanity.

Robespierre told the revolutionary leaders, "The first maxim of your policy ought to be to lead the people by reason and the people's enemies by terror. If the mainspring of popular government in peacetime is virtue, amid revolution it is at the same time virtue and terror: virtue, without which terror is fatal; terror, without which virtue is impotent. Terror is nothing but prompt, severe, inflexible justice; it is therefore an emanation of virtue . . . Does your government, then, resemble a despotism? Yes, as the sword which glitters in the hands of liberty's heroes resembles the one with which tyranny's lackeys are armed."[7]

Evil is not evil when we do it, in other words, because our cause is just so very good.

The British government opposed the radicals. That meant it was getting dangerous to be an Englishman in France. Wordsworth had to get out. He promised Annette he would return. Then he set off for home. But he stopped in Paris first.

There: chaos. The radicals had stormed the Tuileries. They had captured and imprisoned the king. Royalist forces from the continent were invading to stop the revolution's spread. Egged on by Robespierre and his allies, Jacobins went on their first kill-spree: the September Massacres. They slaughtered their political prisoners. In the streets, the cracks between the cobblestones filled with the bubbling blood of thousands, including hundreds of priests.

Wordsworth later recalled he was "pretty hot in it."[8] Apparently, this meant he did some errands for the more peaceful radical Girondists. But eventually, he ran out of money. Reluctantly, he went back to England, leaving Annette and their new baby behind.

It doesn't seem he meant to abandon them forever. Annette's letters to him were always passionate and loving. "Come, my friend, my husband, receive the tender kisses of your wife, of your daughter."[9] She clearly expected him to return and marry her. Maybe he meant to. But he never did. The war kept them apart for twenty-two years. His passion cooled. Life moved on. During Wordsworth's lifetime, the public never learned of his illegitimate daughter in France.

⟨~ᴇ⟩

Back in England, the radical turn of the revolution had brought on a conservative reaction. The government had fears—reasonable fears—that the revolution would spread to their islands and endanger the British monarchy. There was a crackdown. Due process was suspended. Free speech was curtailed. Authors were jailed for their opinions. Protests were shut down.

Depressed, confused, still aimless, and also jobless and penniless, Wordsworth wandered through London, living no one knows how, probably off his friends. Still afire with revolutionary passion, he attended radical meetings. He read radical pamphlets. He nearly got himself in trouble with some writing of his own.

Liberal bishop Richard Watson had been shocked into conservatism by the September Massacres. He delivered a sermon with the marvelously clueless title "The Wisdom and Goodness of God, in Having Made Both Rich and Poor." Wordsworth, outraged, slashed out an angry letter in response. If he'd published it, he almost surely would have been thrown in the slammer. Maybe his friends talked him out of it. Maybe his publisher just quietly filed the thing in his wastebasket. But it never saw the light of day.

Somewhere inside him, though, there had begun the slow-growing realization that the radicals had disgraced their own ideals. What had once seemed to him a "benignant spirit"[10] in the revolution, aimed at eliminating abject poverty and "legalized exclusion,"[11] had given way to tyranny, mass murder, and world war. The oppressed of France had "become oppressors in their turn," he wrote eventually, and, with the rise of Napoleon, they "changed a war of self-defense for one of conquest, losing sight of all which they had struggled for."[12]

As time passed, the years did to Wordsworth what years will do, if you keep your eyes open. They gave him both reasons to become more conservative and the experience to see the wisdom in old ways. His separation from Annette was, I suspect, a godsend. She was too fervent a character to live for long at peace with as large a character as his. The woman he eventually married in 1802, Mary, was a homebody of such quiet serenity that a friend once joked she never said anything except "God bless you!" Wordsworth adored her with a rich and sensual passion. Ten years after their marriage, when they were both forty-two, he wrote to her after they'd been parted for only a few days, telling her about his "fever of thought and longing and affection and desire" for her as he remembered her "limbs as they are stretched upon the soft earth," the "aching of [her] bosom," and her "involuntary sighs and ejaculations."[13] It required both her devotion and the lifelong devotion of his sister, Dorothy, to make a home for a poet whose work was so entirely about his own mind, and whose mind was so entirely in the high hills of the lake country and the clouds above them.

His experience of the failed revolution, his marriage, the birth of his children, the need to make money, the patronage of a local lord—all these pressed him eventually to leave radicalism behind and embrace British tradition and patriotism. The change cost him with many among the intellectual set. What Coleridge called "the clerisy"—the elite, chattering classes who decree what will be the approved opinions of high culture—despised him for his conservative stances. When Wordsworth accepted the post of comptroller of stamps in order to earn his living, Shelley wrote a poem accusing him of "deserting" the causes of "truth and liberty."[14]

But Wordsworth protested, "If I were addressing those who have dealt so liberally with the words *Renegado, Apostate* etc., I should retort the charge upon them & say, *you* have been deluded by *Places & Persons*, while I have stuck to *Principles*."[15] His political enemies were following elite fashion, in other words, whereas he was defending the idea of liberty.

The dramatic shift in Wordsworth's thinking can be traced in the dramatic shift in his attitudes toward Edmund Burke, the Irish Whig who became a member of the British Parliament.[16] In that unpublished letter he wrote to Bishop Watson in his radical days, Wordsworth called Burke an "infatuated moralist" who, in clinging to tradition, was guilty of "a refinement in cruelty superior to that which in the East yokes the living to the dead."[17] But he sounded altogether different in one of his later revisions of the *Prelude*, where he praised Burke specifically because Burke celebrated

> The majesty . . .
> Of Institutes and Laws, hallowed by time;

Declared the vital power of social ties
Endeared by Custom; and with high disdain,
Exploding upstart Theory, insists
Upon the allegiance to which men are born.[18]

Burke has been dead more than two hundred years, but he can still drive radicals to distraction with his simple wisdom. He had the annoying habit of being right about everything. He foresaw American greatness and supported the Americans in their grievances against his own king, George III. He warned Parliament that oppression would drive the Yanks to revolution and begged them to make peace when the revolution came.

But when the French rose up, he predicted early on that terror would follow. His pamphlet condemning the uprising, *Reflections on the Revolution in France*, ignited furious responses from radical republicans—the first one from Mary Wollstonecraft, who issued her pamphlet *A Vindication of the Rights of Men*.

But it was Burke's insights into the virtues of tradition that were vindicated when mass slaughter followed the French revolt, just as he had said it would. Burke understood the great flaw in radical thinking: radicals seek to overturn the very traditions that created their values. As radicals today condemn Thomas Jefferson for holding slaves without realizing they learned their hatred of slavery at Jefferson's knee, so the French slaughtered priests in the love of liberty the church had instilled in them age by painful age. The radical always thinks his pristine morality is what another of Burke's opponents, Thomas Paine, called common sense. But that isn't right. Morality is fashioned in the forge of centuries. It's a thing of iron that will melt away in too much heat.

Burke, by contrast, knew his Aristotle. He understood what

we'll call the paradox of virtue: a society must be virtuous to be free, but it must be free before it can be virtuous because virtue is not virtue unless it is freely chosen.

"It is better to cherish virtue and humanity by leaving much to free will, even with some loss to the object, than to attempt to make men mere machines and instruments of a political benevolence," Burke wrote. "The world on the whole will gain by a liberty without which virtue cannot exist."[19]

It is culture—tradition—that creates a people worthy of freedom, when it grooms them, in freedom, to freely choose the good. The faux virtue of Robespierre, enforced by terror and the guillotine, is no virtue at all. It is oppression and can only create more of itself.

It was not a question of being hidebound. Burke understood that change would come. But he thought change should grow organically from the culture because it was the culture that created the values that demanded the change. In the American colonies, for instance, he saw a people striving to live into their traditions and principles. They were demanding their rights as Englishmen.

But from France, he heard nothing but the high-toned gabble of "a man's abstract right to food or medicine,"[20] which justified murderous oppression and criminality. Universities had become "seminaries" for revolutionary gatherings where, he said sarcastically, "amidst assassination, massacre, and confiscation, perpetrated or meditated, they are forming plans for the good order of future society."[21]

When Queen Marie Antoinette walked with royal dignity and noble calm amid a slavering mob that jeered her to her execution place, Burke understood what had happened. For an abstract idea of liberty, the French had destroyed the fine fabric of tradition on which living liberty rests.

"In a nation of gallant men," he wrote, "in a nation of men of honor, and of cavaliers! I thought ten thousand swords must have leaped from their scabbards, to avenge even a look that threatened her with insult. But the age of chivalry is gone."[22]

Burke praised his fellow Englishmen for their "sullen resistance to innovation."[23] They had learned that trait from hard experience. The English had killed a king of their own not long ago—not a century and a half before the French king and queen were killed— and it had not ended well.

When the English Civil War broke out in 1642, John Milton was a private teacher. He was an erudite, stern, and fussy man. When he was a student at Christ's College, Cambridge, his schoolmates had given him the nickname "The Lady of Christ's" because he wouldn't join them in their whoring.[24] He was a virgin into his thirties.

He was stern and fussy in his religion as well. A Protestant, he fiercely opposed the Catholic practices still remaining in the Church of England and railed against the corruption of its bishops. There was a nickname for that sort of person too: Puritan.

In politics, he sided with the Roundheads against the Cavaliers, the Parliamentarians against the Royalists. Charles I had sought to rule without a parliament. The Parliament had fought to retain its traditional, though unwritten, powers. As the struggle between them became violent, Milton trained with a militia and wrote angry tracts against the church, but he was never in the actual fighting.

When he was thirty-four, as civil war was breaking out, he married a seventeen-year-old girl from a royalist family, Mary Powell. After one month, she left him and returned home. But when it was clear the king was done for, she returned to him, fell on her knees before him, and begged him to take her back. He did—and he gave protection to her and her family during what followed.

After the king's surrender, Milton went to work for the Commonwealth led by Oliver Cromwell. Milton considered Cromwell a champion of liberty, but many since have regarded him as a dictator, and Irish Catholics see him as a genocidal killer. Cromwell's puritan fury against the king helped pave the way for the king's eventual trial and execution.

It was a national trauma as the nobility of tradition met the fever of revolt. As Charles prepared to go to the place of his beheading in January of 1649, he requested two shirts. He didn't want the cold to make him tremble lest the onlookers mistake his trembling for fear. He met his death with kingly calm. As the executioner's axe came down, the onlookers groaned aloud.

—❧

Milton did not sign the king's death warrant, but shortly after Charles was beheaded, the poet did write a treatise justifying the execution. His reasoning was derived from Genesis, making it easy to see the chain of thought that eventually led from the Bible to the American Declaration of Independence:

"No man who knows ought, can be so stupid to deny that all men naturally were born free, being the image and resemblance of God himself, and were by privilege above all the creatures, born to command and not to obey," he wrote.[25] It was only in the ruined world of sin created by "Adam's transgression" that men were forced to band together for self-defense, necessitating the creation of governments and kings. These kings are intended to be restrained by Parliament and bound by law. And most important, their power is given "in trust from the People, to the Common good of them all, in whom the power yet remains fundamentally, and cannot be taken from them, without a violation of their natural birthright." It stands to reason, then, and is confirmed by Scripture, that "the people [may] as oft as they shall judge it for the best, either choose [the king] or reject him, retain him or depose him though no Tyrant, merely by the liberty and right of free born Men, to be governed as seems to them best."[26]

When Cromwell died, his son proved unable to hold the Commonwealth together. In 1660, Charles II, the son of the executed king, returned from exile in Europe to retake the throne. The monarchy was back.

Milton went on the run.

He had no choice. He had approved of Charles I's killing. The penalty for such treason was to be hung, drawn, and quartered. First they hanged you, then they cut you down while you were still alive, then they sliced your genitals off, then they yanked out your bowels and burned them with you watching, then finally they chopped your head off and posted it on a pike, insult to injury. They were not kidding around about this. Several of those who had signed the king's death warrant met this very fate.

To this day, no one knows where Milton went to hide out until things cooled down. It may have been in the home of one of the relations of his late friend, Charles Diodati—the same Diodati family after which the Genovese villa was named, where Mary Shelley conceived of *Frankenstein*.

Milton was a blind man by then—he had gone blind in Cromwell's service. His savings were confiscated. And though he wasn't on any of the lists of those to be executed, there were calls for him to be arrested and for his writings to be burned. What's more, though he was now in his fifties, he had never achieved his dream of literary immortality, that ambition for fame that he called the "last infirmity of noble mind."[27] It was a period of dark danger and disappointment for a stern and fussy man who felt himself capable of greatness and deserving of glory.

At last, after a general pardon was issued, he returned home to live with his three daughters. He treated them shabbily, and they seem to have hated him as a tyrant in return. He taught them how to sound out Latin and Greek so they could read to him in his blindness, but he neglected to teach them the meaning of the words they were reading. "One tongue is enough for a woman," he would say. He was a witty blighter anyhow.

Now, as he lay in bed at night, he began to compose his great work, an epic retelling of Genesis,

> Of Mans First Disobedience, and the Fruit
> Of that Forbidden Tree, whose mortal taste
> Brought Death into the World, and all our woe,
> With loss of EDEN, till one greater Man
> Restore us.[28]

His purpose in writing *Paradise Lost*, he declared grandly, was to "justify the ways of God to men."[29]

Each night, he would memorize the portion he had fashioned in his head. Then, in the morning he would dictate what he had created either to one of his daughters or to a hired scribe. In this way, he produced a work of more than ten thousand lines, the greatest long poem in English, and one of the greatest poems of any kind.

The story is about rebellion: Satan's attempt to overthrow the King of Heaven and Adam and Eve's disobedience to the single edict of God: don't eat the fruit of the tree of knowledge of good and evil.

But Milton did not write *Paradise Lost* as an apology for his role in the Civil War. To his mind, in approving the beheading of his earthly king, he had, after all, sought to serve the heavenly one. C. S. Lewis has it right, I think, in his brilliant *Preface to Paradise Lost*. Milton's poem, Lewis says, is meant to depict that power structure against which no rebellion can succeed: the world's God-made and therefore absolute hierarchy.

The word *hierarchy* originally meant the rule of the sacred, the holy order of things. Milton, says Lewis, "pictures his whole universe as a universe of degrees, from root to stalk, from stalk to flower, from flower to breath, from fruit to human reason."[30] Here, in a harmonious dance, each degree naturally rules the next degree below it, which naturally obeys, and all in love and mutual service: God over Adam, Adam over Eve, "he for God only, she for God in him."

Lewis admits that we in our more egalitarian age may find such hierarchies startling. But he says, "Those who cannot face such startling should not read old books."[31]

For Milton, the conditional echelons of the fallen world— the orders of kings and masters—can be tossed aside if they fail to serve the common good. But he who rebels against God's hierarchy only thinks he will achieve equality and freedom. Without submission to the natural order, there is nothing left but to create new orders by Jacobin force. Rather than the freedom of submission to God's creation, you are left with a world ruled only by power. It is the paradox of virtue knit into the fabric of reality: you will not be free unless you are virtuous; you cannot be virtuous unless you are free.

꩜

What is satanic in Satan's rebellion in *Paradise Lost* is that it is a rebellion against moral reality. Where Wordsworth described a human imagination making new experiences out of the reality it is given—"An agent of the one great Mind . . . working but in alliance with the works which it beholds"—Satan rebels against God in the belief his "unconquerable will" can make of reality whatever it desires.

When God crushes Satan's rebellion and casts him into hell, Satan boasts that he is not defeated, because he brings with him

> A mind not to be changed by Place or Time.
> The mind is its own place, and in it self
> Can make a Heaven of Hell, a Hell of Heaven.[32]

He's wrong. What happens is the exact reverse. Hell slowly transforms Satan's mind into itself. Soon he is crying out:

> Me miserable! which way shall I fly
> Infinite wrath, and infinite despair?
> Which way I fly is Hell; my self am Hell.[33]

Because God's reality *is* reality, there is no way to escape it. Because it is goodness itself, there is no way to defy it with anything but evil. When it comes to the politics of rebellion and change, the rebel can either seek to work in partnership with God's creation or find himself outside it and thus in hell.

Throughout the poem, we watch as Satan insists on his sovereign power to recreate himself however he wishes. His "unconquerable will" will not submit to God's hierarchies. But because those hierarchies are the structure of goodness, he can recreate himself only into lower and lower forms. Rather than rising to become the angel God fashioned him to be, he changes, in Lewis's words, "from hero to general, from general to politician, from politician to secret service agent, and thence to a thing that peers in at bedroom or bathroom windows, and thence to a toad, and finally to a snake."[34]

In his pride, Satan convinces himself it is "better to reign in Hell than serve in Heav'n." That means he can extend his reign only by turning whatever territory he conquers into hell's colony. So, in the form of a snake, he heads for earth to tempt Eve and, through Eve, Adam to seize God's knowledge of good and evil for themselves.

This, finally, is the model of all radicalism, in the grip of which men reenact the fall of man as adults so often reenact their childhood traumas. Radicals transgress the paradox of virtue because they claim the knowledge of good and evil for themselves and strip the power to freely choose virtue from others. In this way, they transform their imagined paradise into a living hell.

Not surprisingly, it was the Romantic radicals who first began to regard Satan as the tragic hero of *Paradise Lost*—as every undergraduate who reads the poem still regards him today. Because they did not believe in God—the author of all good—they could not imagine an absolute power that was not fundamentally abusive. Rebellion against such a power was therefore morally justified. Ipso facto, Satan was a hero.

These Romantics could not read the poem as Milton wrote it and so assumed he wrote it as they read it. Milton "was of the Devil's party without knowing it," William Blake said.

Shelley wrote, "Nothing can exceed the energy and magnificence of the character of Satan as expressed in *Paradise Lost*. It is a mistake to suppose that he could ever have been intended for the popular personification of evil . . . Milton's Devil as a moral being is as far superior to his God as one who perseveres in some purpose which he has conceived to be excellent in spite of adversity and torture, is to one who in the cold security of undoubted triumph inflicts the most horrible revenge upon his enemy."[35]

—⁓—

But Wordsworth, as his radicalism faded, began to see things differently. In his drive to become the new Milton, to create a poem to rival *Paradise Lost*, he sought to reimagine Milton's Christian universe as a psychological map of the soul's interior, in which, says the critic M. H. Abrams, "the heights and depths of the mind of man are to replace heaven and hell."

This was the instinct of genius. Because of course heaven and hell are in the mind of man. The hell we imagine, with its caverns, its torments, its pits of fire, and the heaven we dream of with its fluffy clouds and winged souls playing harps are representative of an actual state of human being that extends from who we are now into eternity. To explore the mind of man is to know the face of damnation and salvation both—to know them in the only way we can know them, a human way, just as we know light and good and evil and the falling silver rain.

~e9~

Wordsworth—lost and dispirited by the failure of the radical project—soon left London for the rural seaside county of Dorset. There, one day in spring, he received a visit from a remarkable man. The man was a genius and a drug addict, a polymath and an overly emotional fool. He was also a Christian with perhaps the most profound and original insight into the Gospels since Aquinas. And he had a preternatural power to ignite the minds of those who knew him with his ideas.

His name was Samuel Taylor Coleridge, and together, in an age of unbelief, he and Wordsworth began to reconstruct the moral imagination of the West.

PART 2

THE JOURNEY
TOWARD SOLUTIONS

CHAPTER 5

THE GATE TO THE GARDEN

Lyrical Ballads *and the Reconstruction of the Soul*

In 1797, on a day in June—one of the most famous days in literary history, though no one seems to know whether it was the 4th or 5th—Samuel Taylor Coleridge walked the forty miles from Somerset to visit Wordsworth at his house in Dorset.

It had been a cold and lingering winter—so cold three stones at Stonehenge, one of the trilithons, two uprights and a lintel, had fallen over because of the heavy frost. But the chilly May had warmed up finally. Dorset's rolling green hills were purple with wildflowers as they ran southward to the sea. It was spring at last.

It was spring in a nation at war. Just that February, the French had landed an invasion force in Wales. It wasn't much of a force. It wasn't much of an invasion. The ragtag band surrendered after only a day or two. Still, the threat was far from over. Napoleon was on the march across the continent. Italy had fallen. Austria had surrendered. Great Britain was becoming isolated. Allies were in short supply. The ships from France might well come again, in full power this time.

Here, in the English countryside, there was bleak poverty all around—poverty and its attendant evils. Every other newborn died. Adults couldn't expect to live past forty. It was no wonder the government was nervous about insurrections, no wonder they were cracking down hard on any talk of revolt.

Both Coleridge and Wordsworth were in the government's sights because of their radicalism. At one point in the coming year, the home office would send a special agent to investigate them. Coleridge would later joke that the agent probably reported their suspicious conversations about "Spy Nozy"—Spinoza.

The truth, though, was that both men were in retreat from political activism. Both were sunk in sorrow and disappointment at how the high-blown dreams of the revolution had given way to such a low and blood-drenched reality. Their hearts were still with the poor, still set on liberty and reform. But each on his own was beginning to turn toward poetry—a new kind of poetry in "the language of men"—as a way of giving voice to the "obscure and lowly" and to the age's yearning for liberation.

⁓𝒆𝄄

Wordsworth, having failed to make his way in London, had seized on a chance to live with his sister, Dorothy, in the country house of a friend. A legacy had come in, and they were also earning some cash by taking care of two children. For a while, at least, their money problems were over.

It was the first time brother and sister had been able to live together since their father died in 1783. The Wordsworth children had been farmed out to various families after that. It had been a long and traumatic separation.

But Wordsworth and Dorothy would never be parted again. Their closeness was to become literary legend. They seemed at times one mind. Her ideas, her observations, even her occasional fine turns of phrase became part and parcel of his poetry. A local farmer would describe how Wordsworth would pace down a pathway muttering new verses to himself—"Bum bum bum"—while "Miss Dorothy kept close behind him and she picked up the bits as he let 'em fall, and tak 'em down, and put 'em on paper for him." Author Adam Nicholson says Dorothy was Wordsworth's "mindsister," a perfect term.[1]

~~~

As for Wordsworth and Coleridge, they had met a few times before over the last year and a half. Coleridge already admired Wordsworth and suspected his genius. "I feel myself a *little man* by his side,"[2] he would say. Wordsworth also suspected Wordsworth's genius. But he hadn't quite wrestled it into the light. He was trying. Pacing the pathway. Bum bum bum.

That June day, working in the garden outside their kitchen, Wordsworth and Dorothy saw Coleridge approach.

"At first I thought him very plain, that is, for about three minutes," Dorothy later remembered. "He is pale, thin, has a wide mouth, thick lips, and not very good teeth, longish, loose-growing, half-curling, rough black hair . . . His eye is large and full, and not very dark, but grey . . . it speaks every emotion of his animated mind."[3]

The main road—the high road—wound around to the front of the house. But as brother and sister watched, Coleridge left the road and—as Wordsworth still remembered more than fifty years later—"Leapt over a gate and bounded down the pathless field," to meet them.[4]

He was twenty-four years old. Wordsworth was twenty-seven.

Already, though, Coleridge was a man who knew everything. He may have been the last man who ever did, the last man who ever could, as this was the last era in which it could be done. Soon, the flourishing sciences and the discoveries of exploration would create uncountable new realms of knowledge that would require specialists to understand them. But for the moment, Coleridge could plausibly daydream about preparing to write an epic poem by first taking ten years to learn "universal science. I would be a tolerable Mathematician. I would thoroughly understand Mechanics, Hydrostatics, Optics and Astronomy, Botany, Metallurgy, Fossilism, Chemistry, Geology, Anatomy, Medicine—then the mind of man— then the minds of men—in all Travels, Voyages and Histories."[5]

In the event, this was only one of the million fantastical ideas that were always going off like fireworks in his brain. Each in turn fluttered down into darkness as his capricious temperament carried his mind off elsewhere and his ever-growing addiction to laudanum rendered him increasingly incapable of focused work.

Still, he never stopped learning. He read everything. And he never stopped talking, either. He talked and talked and talked.

"He talks as a bird sings," said Wordsworth. "As if he could not help it: it is his nature."[6]

"His genius . . . had angelic wings, and fed on manna," wrote William Hazlitt. "He talked on forever, and you wished him to talk on forever. His thoughts did not come with labor and effort; but as if borne on the gusts of genius, and as if the wings of his imagination lifted him from off his feet. His voice rolled on the ear like the pealing organ, and its sound alone was the music of thought. His mind was clothed with wings; and raised on them, he lifted philosophy to heaven."[7]

In that time of genius, Coleridge seemed to be everywhere and to speak to everyone. And everyone he spoke to was changed by what he said.

Charles Lamb first met Coleridge when they were children, both students at the dreary charity school, Christ's Hospital, in London. Coleridge had been sent there when he was eight years old after his beloved father, a vicar, died.

Lamb and Coleridge began a lifelong friendship. Though Lamb's academic career was scuttled by that stutter of his, Coleridge eventually went off to Cambridge. There, says Richard Holmes, he "began to live a kind of double life . . . his wild expenditure on books, drinking, violin lessons, theatre and whoring . . . alternating with fits of suicidal gloom and remorse."[8]

There were debts. There was an absurd effort to escape his debts by joining a cavalry regiment, the King's Light Dragoons. His failed attempts to learn to ride a warhorse left him with saddle sores that "grimly constellated my Posteriors." His brothers eventually got him discharged for reasons of "insanity." There followed an endearingly kooky scheme to start a utopian commune in America, the "Pantocracy." It was another brain flash that faded to nothing. Unfortunately, part of the scheme had involved his getting married to one of the Pantocracy's women. It was a terrible mistake, a cruelly bad marriage for both of them.

During the time he was plotting out this American utopia, he renewed his friendship with Lamb. He returned to London and stayed at an inn called the Salutation and Cat. He and Lamb would meet there and sit by the fire to discuss poetry and politics and their various disappointments in romance.

"He would talk from morn to dewy eve, nor cease till far midnight,"[9] Lamb later remembered. "Yet who would ever interrupt him—who would obstruct that continuous flow of converse."

But this was not entirely a compliment. "From morn to dewy eve" is a phrase from *Paradise Lost*. In the poem, it describes the fall of Satan, his long tumble down from heaven into hell, "from morn to noon . . . from noon to dewy eve, a summer's day." Coleridge, Lamb was saying, could talk like the very devil.

Soon after their meetings at the Salutation and Cat, Lamb had his crack-up and was carted off, delusional, to the madhouse. Lamb's brother blamed Coleridge for it. He thought it was Coleridge's wild conversation that had driven Lamb insane.

Lamb himself remembered Coleridge's chatter as "a blessing partly and partly a curse."[10] When he was recovering from his breakdown, he wrote to Coleridge, "I charge you don't think of coming to see me. Write. I will not see you if you come."[11]

That took place a few years before Coleridge leapt the garden gate at Wordsworth's house. A few years after that, Coleridge visited with radical thinker William Godwin. Godwin's home was always a gathering place for intellectuals and artists. One night, Coleridge recited his great poem there, *The Rime of the Ancient Mariner*. The story goes that Godwin's nine-year-old daughter, Mary, and her stepsister, Claire, hid behind the sofa so they could listen. Claire's mother, Mary's stepmother, ordered the children to bed, but Coleridge pleaded their case and they were allowed to stay and hear the poem through.

Later, when Mary grew up to write *Frankenstein*, she sprinkled references to the *Mariner* throughout the book. Captain Robert Walton, the Arctic explorer who pulls Victor Frankenstein from the icy water, says he learned his love of the sea through reading the *Mariner* by that "most imaginative of modern poets."[12] And when Frankenstein is traveling through the countryside, fearful of meeting his homicidal creation, he uses a quote from the *Mariner* to describe his terror. He says he is

> Like one who, on a lonely road,
> Doth walk in fear and dread,
> And, having once turned round, walks on,
> And turns no more his head;
> Because he knows a frightful fiend
> Doth close behind him tread.[13]

These words from the poem so terrified Mary's lover Shelley that when he first heard them, he fainted dead away.

Fascination and madness, inspiration and fear. The words of Samuel Coleridge had a power to them. They worked on the mind.

For Wordsworth, Coleridge would become a Merlin and a muse. In that first year after he leapt the gate at Dorset, his ideas, his outlook, his endless talk were the conjuring spell that brought Wordsworth's talent to life and to fruition. The book they would write together—*Lyrical Ballads with a Few Other Poems*—would revolutionize the art of English poetry. In doing so, it would give the men and women of this startling new era the words by which to know themselves.

⁓

So what was Coleridge saying then? What was he forever talking about that worked such agitation and such magic on those who heard him?

It's actually not an easy question to answer. Coleridge claimed that he had developed a complete system of philosophy. He always planned to write it down, but of course—of course—he never did. It appears in fragments here and there, in sermons, articles, and dissertations, and in his rambling sort-of-autobiography, *Biographia Literaria*. Sometimes his thoughts are orderly and clear. Often, they are fragmentary and disjointed, the cries of a storm-tossed mind blown to half whispers by interior winds. Always, they are written in the crushingly abstruse style of the German philosophers he loved.

I'm not a German philosopher and, if you've lived your life virtuously, neither are you. All I can do here is set down his ideas as I understand them in the simplest terms I can find. This is bound to sacrifice some precision for clarity and readability, but, in this case, trust me, that's a good deal.

When I was a boy, there was a conundrum popular among

boys my age. "If a tree falls in a forest and there's no one there to hear it, does it make a sound?" I always liked this riddle because I felt it had a meaningful solution. A tree that falls in the forest creates all the necessary *elements* of a sound. But to *be* a sound, there must be someone there to hear it. The listener's ear and brain transform the elements of a sound into a sound in fact. The listener is a creative collaborator in the sound experience. The tree can't make a sound without him, and he can't have the true experience of the sound without the falling tree. He also can't determine what the sound will be. Whether he likes it or not, it will be something in the nature of a splintering crash. In this it is like the rainbow: a collaboration of the human mind and God's creation, unique to each and yet contained, in all, within the boundaries of reality.

But there are other human collaborations with reality that are more complicated. Just as the falling tree creates all the elements of sound but needs the ear to hear it, a sunset creates all the elements of beauty but needs the person who appreciates it. It becomes beauty only when he's there to see it. But what if he doesn't happen to like sunsets? Is it still beautiful, then? What if I commit an act of cruelty but the observer does not find it evil? Is it evil all the same? We can't make the sound of a falling tree into tinkling bells by thinking it's so, but can we make beauty ugliness and evil good? If not, how do we know when our beauty is beauty and our truth is truth?

There is a more relevant sort of collaboration with reality. Let's call it art. Wordsworth describes this in his delightful poem "A Whirl-Blast from behind the Hill."

The poet is in the forest when a hailstorm starts.

> A Whirl-Blast from behind the hill
> Rushed o'er the wood with startling sound;

> Then—all at once the air was still,
> And showers of hailstones pattered round.[14]

Wordsworth takes refuge in a grove surrounded by evergreen holly trees. The forest floor all around him is covered with dead and withered leaves. Wherever the hailstones hit the leaves, the leaves "skip and hop." Wordsworth describes what he witnesses:

> The leaves in myriads jump and spring,
> As if with pipes and music rare
> Some Robin Good-fellow were there,
> And all those leaves, in festive glee,
> Were dancing to the minstrelsy.[15]

In making the leaves jump, the hailstorm creates all the elements of a poem, but it requires a poet, Wordsworth, to see the jumping leaves as a party of fairies dancing to the music of Puck—Robin Goodfellow—the chief sprite of the woods. Now, in writing the poem, Wordsworth has created all the elements of delight, except for us. We now collaborate with him, by taking his imaginative experience into our minds and making it our own. From nature to Wordsworth to us, it is a chain of collaborative creation by which the forest is filled with fairies.

This chain of cocreation is going on every moment we're alive. Trees are falling, the sun is setting, people are acting cruelly and kindly, artists are making books and songs and shows—and we, at every moment, are collaborating with reality to transform these events into sounds and beauty, good and evil, wisdom and delight.

To be a human being is to be a continual work of art.

Now, to take this another step, we return to the movie *Bride of Frankenstein*.

The monster in the picture is, we remember, not the thoughtful Milton-reading wanderer of Mary Shelley's novel but a hulking, grunting brute played by the English actor Boris Karloff in a performance of compassionate genius, one of the greatest performances ever captured on film.

In a famous scene—a scene that is not in the novel—the creature, despised and rejected for his ugliness, comes upon a blind old peasant. The peasant can't see the monster's fearsome appearance, so he welcomes him into his home with kindness. When the peasant realizes his guest has neither language nor any knowledge of civilized life, he begins to teach him. As they share a simple meal, he gives him a lesson.

"This is bread," says the old man, handing a loaf to the monster.

"Bread," repeats the creature. Then he tears into the bread with hilarious animal gusto.

"And this is wine—to drink!" says the peasant.

"Drink," says the monster. And having taken a big sloppy gulp of the wine, he growls, "Good! Good!"

Next, the peasant extends a hand to this reviled and hideous outcast. "We are friends, you and I," the old man says with poignant generosity.

Man and monster happily shake hands, laughing with pleasure. They repeat the words together: "Friend! Good!"

It is a profound moment, a poem of a scene. It illustrates the full chain of cocreation as I think Coleridge understood it.

The scene is filled with biblical echoes. The repetition of the word *good* is meant to remind us of God's creation of the world in Genesis, when he surveys each new wonder he brings into being—light, the sea, the living creatures—and "saw that it was good."[16]

At the same time, we see man and monster collaborating with that creation. They start with one level of collaboration. Like the listener hearing the tree fall and transforming it into sound, the peasant and the creature transform the bread and wine from elements of taste into taste itself. Of the taste their bodies create pleasure and, like God in the days of creation, they declare their pleasure good.

They now move to the next level of collaboration, the spiritual sort that occurs when we see a sunset and call it beautiful, or an act of cruelty and call it evil. The shared meal, the shared company, and the clasped hands become the concept "friendship," and they connect the quality of friendship with the quality of bread and wine: it is a pleasure, it is good. This too is a human creation in collaboration with God's creation. We know this because God declared it is "not good" for a man to be alone.

Finally, of course, we are reminded of another time when the elements of bread and wine are cocreated by human experience from a physical goodness into spiritual goodness—the spiritual goodness of the Logos, the structure of God's creation that God declared was good. This is the rite of the Christian mass, where bread and wine become the flesh and blood of the Logos incarnate, Jesus Christ, the Son of God.

"I have called you friends," Jesus said to his disciples, "for everything that I learned from my Father I have made known to you."[17]

Friend. Good.

One of the most insightful readers of Coleridge's philosophy was English philosopher Owen Barfield, a friend of C. S. Lewis's and, with J. R. R. Tolkien, one of the famous group of Christian writers who called themselves the Inklings. In a wonderful and life-changing little book called *Poetic Diction*, dedicated to Lewis, Barfield explains where poetry fits into the collaborative cycle of creation.

Barfield argues that, in its origins, language originally expressed the unity of physical and spiritual experience. Take, for instance, the word *pneuma*. In Greek, *pneuma* means both "breath" and "spirit." But Barfield thinks these two meanings were once united. People experienced both breath and spirit not as two simultaneous meanings existing together but as one unified thing entirely: *pneuma*, "spirit-breath."

Over time, the meanings became separate in our minds and were related only metaphorically. Without the unity of language, we lost the unity of meaning. It became more difficult for us to experience physical reality as being infused with spiritual meaning.

The purpose of poetry, Barfield says, is to reunite the language of the physical with the language of the spiritual in our minds, and so recreate the original human experience of the physical and the spiritual as one thing. We can see this actually taking place in Wordsworth's poem about the hailstorm. For a moment, in the poet's mind, the withered, dancing leaves become a dance of fairies, the dead forest floor comes to spiritual life.

This is also the purpose of the mass: to make us truly experience bread and wine as body and blood—not two meanings in one but one meaning together. The mass is a kind of poetry, or vice versa. The purpose of both mass and poetry is to remeld the world of flesh and spirit, of things and meaning, into one experience, to regain our original perception of creation, the lost perception of Eden, you might say, before we divided creation into good and evil, back when we saw along with God that it was good.

~e

What happens if we choose not to point ourselves back toward Eden? What happens if we decide that the original experience of creation—flesh and spirit united—was all a fraud, a random accident of the evolutionary brain, a social construct, a false consciousness? That we're just meat puppets animated by chemistry and nothing is either good or bad but thinking makes it so?

That choice—that decision to cease to believe in God's moral universe—is dramatized in Shakespeare's play *Macbeth*. In *Macbeth*, the movie of God's good creation is played in reverse. Instead of Eve being drawn out of Adam so that the interplay of masculine and feminine can bring both into full humanity, Lady Macbeth removes her femininity—"Unsex me here!"[18] she cries—in order to draw her husband out of his humanity altogether so that he might murder his way to the throne of Scotland.

Macbeth and his lady choose to unexperience the moral order, to sever their connection with the Logos and redefine morality from God's good to their own desires. "For my own good," Macbeth says, "all causes shall give way."[19]

Lady Macbeth cannot quite extinguish her inner awareness of God's truth: her conscience. After engineering a spate of murders, she goes mad, trying to wash an imaginary spot of blood from her hand.

But something different happens to Macbeth. In pulling away from God's meaning, he finds he is left with no meaning at all.

Near the end of the play, when he hears of his wife's death and as he faces death himself, he declares his nihilism:

> Life's but a walking shadow, a poor player
> That struts and frets his hour upon the stage
> And then is heard no more: it is a tale
> Told by an idiot, full of sound and fury,
> Signifying nothing.[20]

Shakespeare knows this speech is absurd. Macbeth *is* a player on a stage, and his story not only does not signify nothing, it can't signify nothing. Even if it signifies that life is meaningless, it has that meaning, and so negates its own message. We're back to the old problem of all such relativist philosophies: if there is no truth, how can it be true that there is no truth? If there is no meaning to life, how can the story of life mean there is no meaning? The human mind is a meaning-making machine, and it matters whether we find that meaning in collaboration with reality or step out of that collaboration and find ourselves left with nihilistic nonsense.

That is the point of the speech. Macbeth has *chosen* to separate himself from the Logos. Like Milton's Satan, he thought he had the power to transform evil into good and hell into heaven, but he could only transform himself into evil, and his soul into its own hell.

He forgot that man's experience of life—from the sound of a falling tree to beauty and truth—is a cocreation, a collaboration with God's reality. It is that or it is worse than nothing, it is nothingness.

Which brings us back to the question, How do we know when the creation of our minds is a legitimate cocreation, a collaboration with reality? How do we know our beauty is really beauty and our truth is really truth?

Coleridge found the answer in Jesus. "Might not Christ be the World as revealed to human knowledge?" he asked. "A kind of common sensorium, the total Idea that modifies all thoughts?"[21]

The word *sensorium* means the apparatus of human sensation, the way in which we experience the world. Coleridge's idea is that Christ is the model and perfection of that experience, a true melding of flesh and spirit, life and Logos, man and God. The more we experience the world through Christ, the more we become like Christ and know the world truly. This is what Paul was describing when he said, "It is no longer I who live, but Christ who lives in me."[22]

"In the beginning was the Word [Logos], and the Word was with God, and the Word was God . . . All things were made through Him, and without Him nothing was made that was made. In Him was life, and the life was the light of men . . . And the Word became flesh and dwelt among us."[23]

This is the Gospel of John. This was the faith of Coleridge. He believed in a creator God who expressed his will through the Logos and so made man and nature—man-and-nature, which were one thing, all alive together—and imbued nature with meaning, beauty, and truth that man could discover through the living model of the Logos, Christ. He believed that the human imagination is "a repetition in the finite mind of the eternal act of creation in the infinite I Am."[24]

We are, each of us, the eighth day of creation.

On the day Coleridge arrived in Dorset, Wordsworth had no such certainty. As a young man, he had had moments of dizzying and ecstatic unity with nature, but he had not given that experience a Christian shape. "He venerates Christ and Christianity—I wish he did more," Coleridge said of him.[25] But Coleridge suspected Wordsworth was a "semi-atheist." And though the two of them discussed everything else under the sun, they were "habitually silent" on the subject of religion.[26]

All the same, on that June day Coleridge leapt the gate and came galumphing through the corn rows toward the Wordsworths in their garden, he was bringing his vision to a man who was struggling to find a vision of his own. In the year that followed, Wordsworth and Coleridge—and Dorothy, whom Coleridge would come to call "our sister,"[27]—would walk and talk and write almost as if they were becoming a single imagination.

The Wordsworths ended up moving to Somerset to be nearer the Coleridges. They would climb the rough and beautiful Quantock Hills together, along what today is called The Coleridge Way. Given what we know of Coleridge, it's fair to assume the Wordsworths did a lot of listening, and a lot of pretending to listen as one does with a gabbling child. Nonetheless, like everyone else who ever met Coleridge, Wordsworth could not help but be imbued with the genius of the magnificent mind within this broken man. Wordsworth may have been a semi-atheist in those days, but when later he would describe the poetic imagination as "an agent of the one great mind . . . creator and receiver both, working but in alliance with the works which it beholds,"[28] it is clear that the spirit of Coleridge had spoken into Wordsworth's own spirit. Coleridge had shaped his understanding of the human experience.

The result of their work together was the anthology *Lyrical*

Ballads. By this, I mean the first edition, published in 1798. Later editions included some improvements and many new great and famous poems by Wordsworth, as well as his two important essays on poetry. But as unified works, their shape was, to my mind, distorted by Wordsworth's titanic ego, his attempt to overwhelm and even evict Coleridge's contribution from the original whole. As with everything Coleridge did, his contribution had been as much conversation as content, and that may have annoyed Wordsworth. But Wordsworth was wrong to be annoyed. The original edition had an organic shape that derived from their collaboration, and that shape has a special genius the later editions don't have.

The idea of the book was this. If the purpose of poetry is to reunite flesh and spirit, nature and meaning, through the human imagination, the two poets would approach that purpose from its two opposing poles. Coleridge would bring the imagination of man into nature, and Wordsworth would recreate nature in the image of man's imagination.

As Coleridge described it, he would write about "persons and characters supernatural, or at least romantic; yet so as to transfer from our inward nature a human interest and a semblance of truth sufficient to procure for these shadows of imagination that willing suspension of disbelief for the moment, which constitutes poetic faith."[29] This is where we get the expression "willing suspension of disbelief." It is the process by which the reader sets aside his experience of reality in order to allow the poet's imagination to infuse that reality with spiritual life.

Wordsworth, on the other hand, as Coleridge put it, would "give the charm of novelty to things of every day, and . . . excite a feeling analogous to the supernatural, by awakening the mind's attention from the lethargy of custom, and directing it to the loveliness and the wonders of the world before us."[30] The poet, simply by describing everyday reality as he sees it, would help us overcome our habit of inattention and lift reality up toward its spiritual meanings.

The finished anthology was messier than that neat plan, but you can see the plan in it. The two greatest poems in the volume are the first one, Coleridge's supernatural nightmare, *Rime of the Ancient Mariner*, and the last one, Wordsworth's contemplation of the natural scene a few miles above Tintern Abbey. You can almost read the anthology as a spiritual journey from that first poem to the last.

—❧—

The Rime of the Ancient Mariner begins with the old sailor of the title stopping a man on his way to a wedding. The sailor then tells the wedding guest this tale about a ship he sailed at sea.

The ship was blown into dangerously icy Antarctic waters.

> The Ice was here, the Ice was there,
> The Ice was all around:
> It crack'd and growl'd, and roar'd and howl'd . . .[31]

Suddenly, though, out of the surrounding fog, there appeared a great seabird, an albatross. The sailors hailed it and fed it as if it were "a Christian Soul." It flew around the ship. And, as it did,

> The ice did split with a Thunder-fit;
> The Helmsman steer'd us thro.[32]

Good winds sprang up and drove the ship on its way. The albatross followed. Happily, the crew fed and played with it.

Then, for no reason we ever learn, the mariner, the one telling this story to the waylaid wedding guest, took up his crossbow and shot the albatross dead.

At first, the crew of two hundred men worried that the mariner may have "kill'd the Bird that made the Breeze to blow."[33] But when the sun broke through the fog and mist, they decided, no, killing the bird was a good thing to do.

With that, the wind died completely. The ship was becalmed in strange seas. The crew was surrounded by

> Water, water every where,
> Nor any drop to drink.[34]

Furious with thirst, the crew forced the mariner to wear the albatross around his neck "instead of the Cross."[35]

Now things got really weird. A mysterious ship pulled close to the mariner's. On board were a living skeleton and a woman who looked even more horrifying than he did, with her gold hair and "skin . . . as white as leprosy." The two creatures played dice with each other. The witchy woman cried out, "I've won!" With that, the entire crew of two hundred men fell dead—all except the mariner. In a later edition, Coleridge would explain that the skeleton is "Death" and the woman is the "Night-mare Life-in-Death." Death won the crew. Life-in-Death won the mariner. He will go on living but will be dead inside.[36]

For seven days, the mariner lived on like this, with the dead crew lying all around him.

> Alone, alone, all all alone
> Alone on the wide wide Sea;

> And Christ would take no pity on
> My soul in agony.[37]

The bodies of the dead men stared curses at him from the places where they'd fallen. All around the ship, he saw "slimy things" that "crawl with legs upon the slimy sea."[38]

But when the seven days were over, he experienced a powerful transformation of mind. The slimy snakes on the water somehow began to seem beautiful to him.

> I watch'd their rich attire:
> Blue, glossy green, and velvet black
> They coil'd and swam; and every track
> Was a flash of golden fire.

> O happy living things! no tongue
> Their beauty might declare:
> A spring of love gusht from my heart,
> And I bless'd them unaware![39]

Suddenly, the albatross fell from around his neck. He found himself able to pray. The wind rose. The dead men climbed slowly to their feet. Their animated corpses helped pilot the ship safely back to port. The mariner was rescued, and as he was rowed to shore, the ship behind him was caught up in a vortex and pulled under the waves forever.

With his tale finished, the mariner delivers the moral to the wedding guest:

> He prayeth well who loveth well
> Both man and bird and beast.

> He prayeth best who loveth best,
> All things both great and small:
> For the dear God, who loveth us,
> He made and loveth all.[40]

Having heard the story, the wedding guest goes home to bed and awakes the next day "a sadder and a wiser man."

Aside from the beauty of its language and the nightmare brilliance of its imagery, the genius of the poem lies in the way it locates the Christian mythos in the imagination of man. The senseless killing of the "Christian soul" of the albatross with the crossbow; the fickle passions of the crew like the mob outside Jesus' trial; the interior change of mind that reveals nature through love; the love that frees the mariner to pray so that the body of the bird that hangs around his neck like a cross falls off; the redemption of the dead—it is all as if Coleridge was showing us that even if Christ had never lived, had not been crucified, had not risen from the dead, the truth of his life and crucifixion and resurrection would still be the shape of our perceptions because it is the Logos built into nature. The gospel is the underlying reality of reality and would be murkily apparent in the interplay of nature and our imaginations even if it had not been revealed clearly in history and Scripture.

After the *Rime*, in poem after poem—most of them by Wordsworth—*Lyrical Ballads* shows us the "flash of golden fire" that gives beauty even to "slimy things"—the things we want to turn away from—the poor, the broken, the lowly, the damaged, and the obscure. The poems give us nature irradiated by the interior sensations of the least among us: an abandoned mother who may have killed her child, a female vagrant, a peasant girl in a graveyard who keeps her dead siblings alive in her heart, a forsaken Indian woman, an old man traveling, an idiot boy. Their life, joys, and suffering humanize the hills and forests around. In loving the least of them, we learn to love the nature of which they are a part and we bless creation unawares—without even realizing our hearts have been transformed.

—૯౨

So we come to the final poem in the book, Wordsworth's "Lines Written a Few Miles above Tintern Abbey."

The poet is walking with his "mind-sister" Dorothy on what, in 156 years, will be my birthday, July 13. He comes in view of the abbey, which has been abandoned since the enforced dissolution of the Catholic monasteries during the Reformation. It has fallen into ruins.

Wordsworth's childhood too has fallen—fallen away. He is a disillusioned radical, a great-souled failure. His youthful connection with nature is fading. But—after a year of listening to Coleridge, as the wedding guest listened to the mariner—after incorporating Coleridge's philosophy into his own vision, he is beginning to construct a new approach to life. He is a sadder and wiser man.

"The great poet, in writing himself, writes his time."[41] Wordsworth may be speaking for an entire culture—embodying an entire culture—when he stands by the ruins of Christian unity at the end of Europe's childhood and thinks back to his own childhood and his Edenic connection with the natural world:

> The sounding cataract
> Haunted me like a passion: the tall rock,
> The mountain, and the deep and gloomy wood,
> Their colors and their forms, were then to me
> An appetite; a feeling and a love,
> That had no need of a remoter charm,
> By thought supplied, nor any interest
> Unborrowed from the eye.[42]

He did not need to find philosophy in nature then. He was at one with the simple fact and beauty of it, like a man at the beginning of time who sees breath and spirit as a single thing.

But those days of "aching joys" and "dizzy raptures" and "thoughtless youth" are gone. Now, instead, and as a consolation for their loss, when he looks at nature, and on the entire "mighty world of eye and ear—both what they half create, and what perceive," he hears "the still sad music of humanity" and has "a sense sublime"

> Of something far more deeply interfused,
> Whose dwelling is the light of setting suns,
> And the round ocean and the living air,
> And the blue sky, and in the mind of man:
> A motion and a spirit, that impels
> All thinking things, all objects of all thought,
> And rolls through all things.

In some sense, this Wordsworth, the Wordsworth of "Tintern Abbey," is Coleridge's greatest contribution to the anthology.

To understand the importance of what Coleridge made of Wordsworth and what Wordsworth then created, I'll finish this chapter with a brief story. The story is about John Stuart Mill, the author of *On Liberty*, the great text of classical liberalism, outlining the structures and responsibilities of human freedom.

Mill was born in 1806, eight years after *Lyrical Ballads* was first published. His father was a dour man who, Mill said, took "as the exclusive test of right and wrong, the tendency of actions to produce pleasure or pain."[43] He was a disciple of the philosopher Jeremy Bentham, a utilitarian. Utilitarianism teaches that right action is the action that produces the greatest good for the greatest number of people. It was one of the new and sometimes not-so-new materialist moralities that were gaining popularity as religion faded. Soon, there would also be Marxism, capitalism, evolutionism, Freudianism, and others—each perhaps with something worthy to say about the human condition, but each fatally flawed as a means of establishing a truly moral system. Today, there is evolutionary biology, which is also contributing to our understanding and which will also ultimately fail as a source of moral wisdom.

Mill's father raised him in an experimental manner—a "scientific" manner, as it were. He punished his son and rewarded him specifically in order to cause his mind to associate pleasure with those things which would benefit society and pain with those things which would not. The precocious Mill learned the lesson and grew up, he would write, passionately determined to be "a reformer of the world."[44]

But when he was in his twenties, something happened to him. He asked himself a question: "Suppose that all your objects in life were realized; that all the changes in institutions and opinions which you are looking forward to, could be completely effected at this very instant: would this be a great joy and happiness to you?"[45]

The answer came back to him: no.

With that, the entire purpose and foundation of his life collapsed. His upbringing had been a lie. He had been taught to associate pleasure with being a reformer, but even if he reformed all, he knew there would be no pleasure in it. How could he bring happiness to humanity if he could not even bring it to himself? He was plunged at once into a terrible crisis of depression.

What cured him was reading Wordsworth.

"What made Wordsworth's poems a medicine for my state of mind, was that they expressed, not mere outward beauty, but states of feeling, and of thought colored by feeling, under the excitement of beauty . . . In them I seemed to draw from a source of inward joy."[46]

This inward joy, he realized, was a true purpose, and a purpose available not just to himself but to all people independent of their ambitions and endeavors.

His depression left him and never returned.

The accomplishment of Wordsworth and Coleridge was to answer the question that opens *Hamlet*: Who's there? By depicting the human imagination as "a repetition in the finite mind of the eternal act of creation in the infinite I Am,"[47] and as "an agent of the one great mind . . . creator and receiver both, working but in alliance with the works which it beholds,"[48] they had restored the essentially Christian relationship of man with the Logos. They had written a new mass, which made of all nature the bread and wine, the melding of material and meaning.

Which brings us back to C. S. Lewis's observation: "For some souls I believe, for my own I remember, Wordsworthian contemplation can be the first and lowest form of recognition that there is something outside ourselves which demands reverence . . . For 'the man coming up from below' the Wordsworthian experience is an advance. Even if he goes no further he has escaped the worst arrogance of materialism: if he goes on he will be converted."[49]

For now, the name of Christ was silent. In this increasingly irreligious age, the poets had woven him invisibly into the interplay of nature and the imagination. For now, skeptics like Mill were not asked to believe in God or religion but only, in the words of the psalm, to "taste and see that the Lord is good."[50]

It might be that in the end this strategy would undermine Romanticism as a fully reasoned approach to life. It might be there would come a time when, in order to experience the inward joy the Romantics offered, we would be compelled by force of logic to confront the infinite I AM and ask ourselves the old question, Can we believe?

But for now, in this hinge of history, at the start of the crisis of unbelief, for men like Mill and all the men like Mill who followed, the poets had found a way to reconstruct the human soul.

CHAPTER 6

THE SONGS OF SPRING

Keats's Odes and Reconstructing Eternity

Twenty years after Coleridge leapt the gate to come to Wordsworth's house, Wordsworth came to Haydon's house for the Immortal Evening. Coleridge was in London too that day—so was Shelley—but they had not been invited.

Coleridge was a ruin by then, broken and addicted—pitiful, as all literary England knew. He and Wordsworth had grown apart. They had even feuded for a while—about a million things and about nothing.

There had been Wordsworth's annexation of *Lyrical Ballads*: a new edition with Wordsworth's work nearly crowding out Coleridge's contribution. Coleridge, who always idolized Wordsworth, couldn't bring himself to object. But his friends knew he had been slighted, and he must have known as well.

Then there had been Coleridge's hysterical and unrequited

passion for Wordsworth's sister-in-law, Sara. Coleridge was tormented by the time he saw—or had he dreamed?—Wordsworth in bed with Sara with "her beautiful breasts uncovered."[1]

"Must I not be beloved near him except as a Satellite?" he wrote frantically in his diary. "But O mercy, mercy! Is he not better, greater, more manly, and altogether more attractive to any but the purest Woman? And yet . . . he does not pretend, he does not wish, to love you as I love you, Sara!"[2]

Whether this tryst between Wordsworth and his wife's sister really happened or not, it's impossible to tell. Even Coleridge, in his drugged and often drunken state, wasn't completely sure he hadn't imagined it.

Then there was a remark that Wordsworth made to a friend, saying he had "no hope" of rescuing Coleridge from the depths of his addiction.[3] The comment got back to Coleridge. It broke his frenzied heart.

Whatever the reasons, some sort of breach between the two had always been inevitable. Coleridge was no good at life. Wordsworth was. He was disciplined, self-confident, and careful of his responsibilities to his family. When Coleridge went into his vicious downward spiral, Wordsworth could not and would not go along for the ride.

The two had made up the worst of their feud. All that Christmas season—the season of the Immortal Evening—they had appeared at parties together. Their relations seemed friendly, but strained. Coleridge could still command a room with his mesmerizing and mystic chatter, whereas Wordsworth, according to Keats, "left a bad impression wherever he visited in town by his egotism, Vanity, and bigotry."[4] At one dinner party, at Charles Lamb's house, Coleridge was seen in a group of his admirers reciting Wordsworth's poetry, while Wordsworth was seen in a group of his admirers—also reciting Wordsworth's poetry!

The spiritual meld of minds that had brought *Lyrical Ballads* into being was over.

Keats had also idolized Wordsworth and was also moving away from him. Wordsworth's disparaging remark about Keats's first long poem *Endymion*—"a very pretty piece of Paganism"—had cut him to his heart.[5] And Wordsworth's ossifying worldview—"his egotism, Vanity, and bigotry"—had put him off.[6] He began to reconsider his admiration of the older poet's work.

"It may be said that we ought to read our contemporaries, that Wordsworth, etc., should have their due from us," he wrote grumpily at the end of Wordsworth's London visit. "But, for the sake of a few fine imaginative or domestic passages, are we to be bullied into a certain Philosophy engendered in the whims of an Egotist? Every man has his speculations, but every man does not brood and peacock over them till he makes a false coinage and deceives himself."[7]

Keats had already begun to feel there was a higher level of poetic temperament, an artistic point of view that went beyond the self-certainties in Wordsworth's "egotistical sublime."[8] There was, he wrote, a quality that "went to form a Man of Achievement, especially in Literature, and which Shakespeare possessed so enormously—I mean Negative Capability, that is, when a man is capable of being in uncertainties, mysteries, doubts, without any irritable reaching after fact and reason."[9]

In this revolutionary age, in this age of forming philosophies, taking sides, and declaring positions, Keats began to feel that "the only means of strengthening one's intellect is to make up one's mind about nothing—to let the mind be a thoroughfare for all thoughts, not a select party."

As a poet, he wanted to delight in the whole of creation, "foul or fair, high or low, rich or poor, mean or elevated." And to do this, he wanted to develop a "poetical Character," larger than any opinion or philosophy, so large it almost vanished into the all-in-all.[10]

"It is not itself—it has no self—It is everything and nothing—It has no character—it enjoys light and shade; it lives in gusto."

~ϱ~

In the years after the Immortal Evening, Keats struggled toward this far-off vision against a rising tide of disappointment, vexation, and grief.

His younger brother, George, emigrated to America, leaving him to deal with the family's complex and difficult financial situation alone. And, though no one could quite admit it, his youngest brother, Tom, was very ill. The cheerful eighteen-year-old did everything he could to put on a show of gaiety and optimism, but he had tuberculosis. He was dying.

Keats's own health was delicate too. He had a bad habit of traveling on the outside of coaches to save money. He was always catching cold and fighting sore throats.

Then there was the publication of *Endymion* in March 1818. It was a disaster. The critics brutalized him. Conservative journals were especially cruel. They associated Keats with his radical friend Leigh Hunt, though Keats himself was not really very political at all. The reviewer at *Blackwood's*, who had discovered that Keats had trained as an apothecary and surgeon, delivered the famously dismissive advice, "Back to the shop, Mr. John, back to the 'plasters, pills, and ointment boxes,' etc. But, for Heaven's sake . . . be a little more sparing of extentuatives and soporifics in your practice than you have been in your poetry."[11]

An even nastier and more influential attack came from John Wilson Croker of the *Quarterly Review*. He was a critic known for his vicious pettiness. William Hazlitt called him "the talking potato."[12] But he was powerful enough to do serious damage to Keats's career.

"We have made efforts almost as superhuman as the story itself appears to be, to get through it," Croker wrote of the poem, "but with the fullest stretch of our perseverance, we are forced to confess that we have not been able to struggle beyond the first of the four books of which this Poetic Romance consists."[13]

Keats's literary friends rallied round and wrote responses. Keats himself—struggling with George's departure and Tom's worsening illness and his own sore throat—tried to take a high-minded tone.

"[*Endymion*] is as good as I had power to make it," he wrote to a friend. "Had I been nervous about its being a perfect piece, and with that view asked advice, and trembled over every page, it would not have been written . . . The Genius of Poetry must work out its own salvation in a man . . . I was never afraid of failure; for I would sooner fail than not be among the greatest."[14]

It was a lofty sentiment. He probably meant it too. But emotionally, the poem's harsh reception was a blow. When his health began to deteriorate, many of his friends would blame the savagery of the critics.

But Keats wrote on. His work grew better, deeper, richer. He began a new epic, *Hyperion*. He labored at it as he sat beside his brother's sickbed. That's what he was doing in December of that year when Tom finally passed away.

"The last days of poor Tom were of the most distressing nature," he wrote to George in America, "but his last moments were not so painful, and his very last was without a pang. I will not enter into any parsonic comments on death—yet the common observations of the commonest people on death are as true as their proverbs. I have scarce a doubt of immortality of some nature or other—neither had Tom."[15]

Now Keats, twenty-three, grappled with the specter of mortality. He began to see the world as a "Vale of Soul-Making," a school of "pains and trouble," that transformed the heart into "the mind's Bible . . . the text from which the Mind or Intelligence sucks its identity." Through suffering "does God make individual beings, Souls, Identical Souls of the sparks of his own essence."[16]

But suffering—his brother's death, money troubles, the rejection of the critics, and the blow to his dreams of literary greatness—had wounded him deeply. His work began to dry up. He couldn't finish *Hyperion*. He wondered whether he should take *Blackwood's* advice and return to medicine, perhaps train as a physician. "It's not worse than writing poems, and hanging them up to be fly-blown on the Review shambles," he wrote his brother George.[17] A *shambles* is a butcher's stall. He felt *Endymion* had been hung up like a slab of beef and devoured by flies. He could not face a repeat of that failure.

Winter turned into the spring of 1819—as famous a spring

as any in the history of English poetry. Keats continued wandering in his mental wilderness of sorrow and stagnation. He was mourning—his brother and his career. He couldn't write. His sore throat had returned and now a worrying, persistent cough came with it. Had he caught consumption from Tom?

"Neither Poetry, nor Ambition, nor Love" could stir him from his depression and indolence.[18]

Then, one Sunday afternoon in April, he was walking across Hampstead Heath toward Highgate. He was "in the lane that winds by the side of Lord Mansfield's park" when he saw two men approaching him.[19] One of them he knew personally: it was the surgeon, Joseph Henry Green, who had taught him during his medical training.

The other was a shambling, white-haired figure: Samuel Coleridge.

Green introduced the two poets. They walked together on the lane. Moving at a slow pace, side by side, they traveled about two miles. The walk lasted maybe forty-five minutes to an hour. During all that time, Coleridge never once stopped talking.

Keats wrote his brother George about the interchange. The description is priceless:

"In those two Miles he broached a thousand things—let me see if I can give you a list—Nightingales—Poetry—on Poetical Sensation—Metaphysics—Different genera and species of Dreams—Nightmare—a dream accompanied by a sense of touch—single and double touch—a dream related—First and second consciousness—the difference explained between will and Volition—so say metaphysicians from a want of smoking the second consciousness—Monsters—the Kraken—Mermaids—Southey believes in them—Southey's belief too much diluted—a Ghost story—Good morning—I heard his voice as he came towards me—I heard it as he moved away—I had heard it all the interval—if it may be called so. He was civil enough to ask me to call on him at Highgate. Good-night!"[20]

Keats never did call on him at Highgate. This was the one and only time he was vouchsafed the Coleridge Experience, that overwhelming flood of genius as the great and unhappy man poured out his visionary monologue. Here was the font of words that drove Lamb mad, that inspired Mary Shelley, that made Percy Shelley faint away, that turned Wordsworth into the poet he was meant to be.

And now, talking every second, he reached into the darkness of Keats's sorrow as with a holy hand and drew the young poet out into a radiant explosion of creation.

Over the next two months, Keats would produce, in rapid fire one after another, five odes, sometimes called the Odes of Spring, followed by a sixth ode in September. They are some of the greatest poetry ever written, the greatest written in English since Shakespeare.

What had Coleridge said to Keats about nightingales? The birds were all around the heath that spring, "incessant with song," Coleridge remarked.[21]

It was a song associated with sorrow. The nightingale was

linked in classical mythology to the metamorphosis of Philomela. As the story went, she had been raped by Tereus, the hot-blooded king of Thrace. To keep her from exposing the crime, he cut out her tongue. She was ultimately transformed into the nightingale, whose strange song—"Most musical, most melancholy," Milton said—is supposed to echo her attempts to speak her rapist's name.[22]

But Coleridge would not accept the myth—neither the myth nor the melancholy. In a poem on the nightingale for *Lyrical Ballads*, he declared, "In Nature there is nothing melancholy." For a poet to impose his own sadness on the bird is to "profane Nature's sweet voices, always full of love and joyance!" Instead, he says, poets should surrender their whole spirits to nature so that they may "share in Nature's immortality."[23]

So then, a week or two after his walk with Coleridge in the park, here was Keats, steeped in grief, struggling to ignite his genius, sitting in the deep darkness of a Hampstead garden, when he heard a nightingale sing.

The bird in Keats's "Ode to a Nightingale" is a Coleridge creature. It is not melancholy at all, but the singer of the joyful song of nature's immortality, free from

> The weariness, the fever, and the fret
> Here, where men sit and hear each other groan;
> Where palsy shakes a few, sad, last gray hairs,
> Where youth grows pale, and specter-thin, and dies;
> Where but to think is to be full of sorrow
> And leaden-eyed despairs,
> Where Beauty cannot keep her lustrous eyes,
> Or new Love pine at them beyond to-morrow.

But sad as he is, sitting there in the dark, how can Keats take Coleridge's advice and surrender his spirit to nature's eternal song? At first, he wishes he could get drunk enough to lose himself in the music. But he rejects that idea and decides that he will reach out to the bird, as Coleridge recommends, through his poetic imagination.

What he imagines is his own death, and for a moment, he does seem to vanish into the nightingale's trill as it comes to him through both history and fantasy:

> Thou wast not born for death, immortal Bird! . . .
> The voice I hear this passing night was heard
> In ancient days by emperor and clown:
> Perhaps the self-same song that found a path
> Through the sad heart of Ruth, when, sick for home,
> She stood in tears amid the alien corn;
> The same that oft-times hath
> Charm'd magic casements, opening on the foam
> Of perilous seas, in faery lands forlorn.[24]

But the experience lasts only a moment. The word *forlorn* is like "a bell to toll me back from thee to my sole self!" Keats is left alone with his grief in the dark again, disappointed to realize that the imagination "cannot cheat so well as she is fam'd to do," and won't lift him for long out of his suffering and mortality.

This is a very different—more tragic—idea of nature than the one in *Lyrical Ballads*. In the ballads, nature is "always full of love and joyance," as Coleridge says. She leads the heart that loves her, in Wordsworth's words, "from joy to joy." But for Keats, suffering stands like a bolted door between the mortal darkness where the poet sits and the eternal fairy radiance around the nightingale, where "tender is the night."

~~~

In "Ode on a Grecian Urn," Keats repeated this melancholy motion out of himself into an unreachable forever and back into his suffering mortality. Here, eternity is not embodied in natural music that travels through time. The ancient urn—with its man-made carvings of maidens being chased by lovers, a piper piping, a heifer being led to sacrifice—is also a song of sorts, but a silent song that never changes. As Keats tells the carved figures,

> Bold Lover, never, never canst thou kiss,
> Though winning near the goal yet, do not grieve;
> She cannot fade, though thou hast not thy bliss,
> For ever wilt thou love, and she be fair!
>
> Ah, happy, happy boughs! that cannot shed
> Your leaves, nor ever bid the Spring adieu;
> And, happy melodist, unwearied,
> For ever piping songs for ever new;
> More happy love! more happy, happy love!
> For ever warm and still to be enjoy'd . . .

As Keats thinks these thoughts, the scene comes to life in his mind. He hears the heifer lowing at the skies and senses some unseen town emptied of its people as they rush to attend the sacrifice. He has imagined himself into the urn's static eternity.

Then, as with the nightingale, the moment is over. He returns to his "sole self," and the urn subsides into a "Cold Pastoral" that will survive his death to go on and speak to others in the future.

> When old age shall this generation waste
> Thou shalt remain, in midst of other woe
> Than ours, a friend to man, to whom thou say'st,
> "Beauty is truth, truth beauty,—that is all
> Ye know on earth, and all ye need to know."[25]

This beauty that is truth is not mere prettiness, not just things we find attractive. It is the nexus of the imagination with the eternally real. Keats had once compared such beauty to the loveliness of Eve in *Paradise Lost*. Adam dreamed about her, then awoke and found that she was truly there. In the same way, what the imagination at its most sublime makes beautiful—even if it didn't exist before—becomes the living representative of an immortal truth beyond itself.

Art can communicate that immortal truth, but like the song of the nightingale, it ultimately leaves us behind in our world of suffering.

Nature and art may be eternal, full of love and joyance, traveling from joy to joy. The imagination can link us to that immortality for a moment. But ultimately, we are tolled back forlornly to our sole selves, where beauty fades, where youths like Tom grow pale and specter-thin and die, where but to think upon these things is to be full of sorrow.

❧

The last of these odes was the one Keats wrote in September, "To Autumn." It seems to have come to him in a moment. "How beautiful the season is now—How fine the air," he wrote to a friend. "This struck me so much in my Sunday's walk that I composed upon it."

He had been rambling by the River Itchen in Winchester past stubble fields beyond the medieval Saint Cross hospital. The ode he wrote is often called a perfect poem. I think it is. It may not have the tragic depth of "Nightingale" or "Grecian Urn," but, more than any poem I can think of, it does what Coleridge thought poems should do: it shares "in Nature's immortality" and makes "all Nature lovelier."[26]

Here, there is no out-and-back motion as in the other odes. The poet, the mortal observer, Keats, has vanished into the scenery completely. We are simply in that imaginative instant when his mind and the world become a single thing: autumn, the season on the borderland of fullest life and death.

There are three verses.

The first is a vision of complete ripeness in the "season of mists and mellow fruitfulness," the season that conspires with the sun

> To load and bless
> With fruit the vines that round the thatch-eves run;
> To bend with apples the moss'd cottage-trees,
> And fill all fruit with ripeness to the core;
> To swell the gourd, and plump the hazel shells
> With a sweet kernel; to set budding more,
> And still more, later flowers for the bees,
> Until they think warm days will never cease.

In the second verse, the season becomes personified. Keats sees autumn

> Sitting careless on a granary floor,
> Thy hair soft-lifted by the winnowing wind.

In the final verse, the poet celebrates the season even as sundown settles in to hint of death. Death is contained within the very ripeness of the season. Full-blown, it whispers of the end of things.

> Where are the songs of Spring? Ay, where are they?
> Think not of them, thou hast thy music too,—
> While barred clouds bloom the soft-dying day,
> And touch the stubble-plains with rosy hue.[27]

The poem is so complete unto itself there is almost nothing to say about it. It's like a Shakespeare play—you make of it what you make of life. But here's what comes into my mind. Keats sees the process of life and death here as one process, life-and-death in a timeless Now. And when he sees it fully and enters it fully, it becomes personified: it has a human face.

This same thing happens too, I think, in one of the most profound and important scenes in all of literature: Moses before the burning bush. Like autumn, the bush contains life-and-death in a single eternal process, the growing bush never consumed by the destructive fire that never dies. Like autumn, the bush, when Moses looks at it, reveals itself to be a person: I AM.

As Keats had written in an earlier letter, "What the Imagination seizes as Beauty must be truth—whether it existed before or not."[28] It is as if he had begun to suspect—to feel, to sense, to imagine—that there was a realm beyond nature, a living reality that nature only symbolized.

I can't help but wonder what Keats—with his brilliant

speculations about earthly life as a vale where suffering makes souls of us, and with his certain sense that that soul has "immortality of some nature or other"—I can't help but wonder what he would have come to see and experience as his poetic imagination reached its own ripeness and the fruition of its wisdom.

But we'll never know.

—❧—

That two-mile walk Keats took with Coleridge—that walk that must have lasted forty minutes to an hour—Coleridge remembered it as lasting only "a minute or so." That was probably because he never stopped talking.[29]

He remembered how, when the walk was over, he and Keats stood together with Green, the doctor they both knew. Then Keats began to leave. But after a few steps, he turned back to the others. He said, "Let me carry away the memory, Coleridge, of having pressed your hand!"

They shook hands. Then Keats walked away.

Coleridge turned to Green and said, "There is death in that hand."[30]

By February of the next year, the signs were unmistakable. A sore throat that never healed. A persistent cough. Harried by increasing money troubles, shaken by a passionate but fraught engagement with a young woman named Fanny Brawne, Keats, with his medical training, had begun to suspect the worst.

He was living then with his businessman friend Charles Armitage Brown in a house in Hampstead. One night, he rode home—as he too often did—on the outside of a coach. He stumbled into the house, said Brown, "in a state that looked like fierce intoxication. Such a state in him I knew was impossible; it therefore was the more fearful. I asked hurriedly, 'What is the matter? You are fevered?' 'Yes, yes,' he answered, 'I was on the outside of the stage this bitter day, till I was severely chilled—but now I don't feel it. Fevered—of course, a little.' He was easily persuaded to go to bed; and, as he leapt into the cold sheets, before his head was on the pillow, he slightly coughed and said: 'That is blood from my mouth. Bring me the candle, let me see this blood!' He gazed steadfastly some moments at the ruddy stain, and then, looking up with an expression of sudden calmness never to be forgotten, said, 'I know the color of that blood; it is arterial blood; I cannot be deceived in that color; that drop of blood is my death-warrant, I must die!'"[31]

So began what Keats would come to call his "posthumous existence,"[32] a dying time beyond poetry and beyond the long descriptive letters that are among his best works. He produced almost nothing in this period but his own life story.

That summer, his last book was published. Keats said it would be his final attempt at literary success. If it failed, he said, "I shall try what I can do in the Apothecary line."[33] The first reviews were good, but the sales were not. It was as great a collection of poems as has ever been written, but he never knew.

"If I should die," he wrote sadly to Fanny, "I have left no immortal work behind—nothing to make my friends proud of my memory—but I have loved the principle of beauty in all things, and if I had had time I would have made myself remembered."

Soon after, his doctors told him he had to move to a warmer climate or he would die. He made plans to sail for Italy. At the last moment, his casual acquaintance, aspiring painter Joseph Severn, was convinced to accompany him. Severn was a timid fellow and a bit of a hysteric, but he endeared himself to literary history and to any feeling heart by bravely—and sometimes not so bravely—sticking by the young poet and nursing him through his last terrible months.

After a dreadful sea voyage, the two men found a set of rooms in Rome. Out the window was the sweep of the Spanish Steps with the graceful Fountain of the Old Boat at the bottom.

Keats's illness grew worse. The fight for breath and the stomach pains were awful. Awful too was his certainty—false though it was, false as anything could be—that he had failed in all he'd hoped for. He had wanted so much—so much—to be counted "among the English poets."[34] Instead, he had encountered nothing but rejection and humiliation. *Back to the shop, Mr. John!* He did not know—had no idea—what he had achieved. He was dying in a torment of despair.

"This noble fellow lying on the bed—is dying in horror," Severn wrote to a friend. "No kind hope smoothing down his suffering—no philosophy—no religion to support him—yet with all the most gnawing desire for it . . . For he says in words that tear my very heartstrings—'miserable wretch I am—this last cheap comfort . . . is deny'd me in my last moments—why is this—O! I have serv'd every one with my utmost good—yet why is this—I cannot understand this.'—and then his chattering teeth."[35]

As death drew near, Keats lay listening to the plash and trickle of water in the fountain below. Words from an old play kept coming into his mind: "All your better deeds shall be in water writ." He told Severn he wanted no name or epitaph on his grave, but only the words, "Here lies one whose name was writ in water."[36]

Finally, toward the end of February, Severn wrote, "the approaches of death came on."

Keats called for him, "Severn—I—lift me up." Severn lifted

him in his arms. Keats told him, "I am dying—I shall die easy—don't be frightened—be firm, and thank God it has come!"

He lay like that a few more hours. Then, Severn later wrote, "He died with the most perfect ease—he seemed to go to sleep."[37]

The death of a poet—a young poet especially—especially one who had been ignored or maligned by the critics—was already a subject that haunted the Romantic mind. Seventeen-year-old Thomas Chatterton had killed himself in obscurity in 1770, after failing to make a living with his poetry and political writings. Wordsworth, Coleridge, Shelley, and Keats had all written about him. The general idea was that, though the poet should die scorned by the world, yet shall he live in his immortal works.

Keats had written of Chatterton, "Thou art among the stars of highest heaven."[38]

And Coleridge had prayed to Chatterton's spirit for poetic inspiration:

> Grant me, like thee, the lyre to sound,
> Like thee, with fire divine to glow—[39]

In the case of Keats, his literary friends and fellow poets had a sense that he had been martyred by the cruelty of the critics.

"To say that his death was caused by the Review is absurd," wrote Coleridge. But Coleridge had suffered at the hands of the critics too and he added, "At the same time it is impossible adequately to conceive the effect which it must have had on his mind."[40]

Byron, famous from his youth, could afford to be more droll about such matters. But he connected Keats's death with the attack from *Blackwood's*. In his satirical epic *Don Juan*, he wrote of "Keats, who was killed off by one critique," and remarked,

> 'Tis strange the mind, that fiery particle,
> Should let itself be snuffed out by an article.[41]

But it was Shelley—according to his biographer Richard Holmes—Shelley, whose work had also been attacked and rejected, who not only could not find an audience but also lived so often in the shadow of the famous Byron—it was Shelley who poured his "terrible bitterness against reviewers"[42] into "Adonais," his beautiful elegy for Keats, which begins, "I weep for Adonais—he is dead!"

In "Adonais," Keats's death is a final release from the illusions of life into the full reality of the spirit:

> The One remains, the many change and pass;
> Heaven's light forever shines, Earth's shadows fly;
> Life, like a dome of many-colour'd glass,
> Stains the white radiance of Eternity.[43]

Keats—Adonais—was now "made one with Nature," and his poetic voice was "in all her music, from the moan of thunder, to the song of night's sweet bird; He is a presence to be felt and known in darkness and in light." He is "a portion of the loveliness which once he made more lovely," and "the soul of Adonais, like a star, Beacons from the abode where the Eternal are."[44]

It is as if Keats had once again gone out of himself into an imagined realm of immortal love and joyance, only this time, finally, never to return.

—ౕ—

A year and a half after Keats died, Shelley, twenty-nine years old, drowned when his sailboat sank in a storm on the Gulf of La Spezia. When his body washed ashore, he had a copy of Keats's final volume of poems in his pocket.

Byron was there when they cremated him on the beach at Viareggio, a single seabird crying overhead. He couldn't bear to watch the body burn. So he threw off his clothes and swam out into the Tyrrhenian Sea. "I never met a man who wasn't a beast in comparison," he said of Shelley—maybe the nicest thing he ever said about anyone.

From that time on, Mary and others went to work rewriting Shelley's reputation, transforming him from a neurotic atheist radical, which he was, to an ethereal angel of high verse, which at times he also was.

Two years after Shelley drowned, Byron died at thirty-six. Fighting vainly the old ennui, as Cole Porter might have said, he had joined the Greek battle for independence from the Ottoman Empire. He had been helping to plan a siege on Lepanto when he contracted his fatal illness. Alfred Tennyson, who would become the great English poet of the Victorians, was fourteen at the time. When he heard the news, he later said, "It seemed an awful calamity. I remember I rushed out of doors, sat down by myself, shouted aloud, and wrote on the sandstone, 'BYRON IS DEAD!'"[45]

Wordsworth and Mary Shelley lived on. They both became staid Victorians and saw the age of social and political revolution morph into a time of sexual restraint, measured reform, exploration, and empire: the pinnacle of the British Century.

~ℯ~

It is often said that the Romantic generations failed in their underlying mission "to create a new world on the ruins of the old." They had tried "to salvage traditional values and the traditional hope for a new earth from the dissolving creeds which had hitherto been their source and sanction."[46] But without the sanction of those creeds—without the full sense of a realm beyond nature, a realm of truth that nature only represents—their system could not stand. Only Coleridge was philosophically brilliant enough to understand that their declarations about nature—its immortality, its beauty and truth—needed to rest upon the supernatural, "a kind of common sensorium"—as he called Jesus Christ—"the total Idea that modifies all thoughts."

But Coleridge's spirit was too great for his body to contain it. He ruined himself before he could say what he meant to say. Wordsworth found religion in the end, but the talent of his youth by then was gone. Keats, for a single season, seemed to stand upon an imaginative height and see a greater truth in the distance, but if he was headed toward that promised land, he was not allowed to enter in.

Sometimes in my more fanciful moments, I see these three as a sort of half-realized imitation of the thing they were seeking. I see Wordsworth as the Logos-begetting Father; Keats as the Son who gave that Logos life in his final poems and who was then martyred and finally resurrected in the fame he never knew he won; and

Coleridge as the Not-So-Holy Spirit moving between them both. They are like a ruined statue of the Trinity in some abandoned Forum in the imagination of the West, a relic of the fallen empire of Christendom.

~~

But those are just the mortal men, long gone. The poetry is the thing that lives, and I don't think it was a failure at all. I think it was a beginning.

Great poets are not prophets, but they somehow are. "The great poet, in writing himself, writes his time," to quote Eliot once again. In writing his time, he writes the future that his time implies. These men—and Mary Shelley too—foresaw the mind of materialism coming, a mind with its spirit gone, the mind we have today. As Wordsworth said then, we could say more loudly now:

> The world is too much with us; late and soon,
> Getting and spending, we lay waste our powers;
> Little we see in Nature that is ours;
> We have given our hearts away . . .[47]

Their poetry is a pilgrim road, a strait and narrow path toward a place we half-remember but never really knew. The poetry does not speak of Christ, but Coleridge was right, it depends on him, it comes out of him, and, read properly, I think it brings us back to him, sadder and wiser for having traveled through the wilderness to reach his throne.

Read properly, I think the poetry of the Romantics is like that journey their last disciple, T. S. Eliot, speaks of, that journey that takes us back to where we started so that we can know the place for the first time.

Having seen, then, what we've seen, knowing now what we know, let us move on to the Gospels with the philosophy of the Romantics in mind.

PART 3

RECONSTRUCTING JESUS

CHAPTER 7

A ROMANTIC MEDITATION ON THE GOSPELS

1. THE WORD MADE FLESH: JESUS VERSUS UNBELIEF

In the beginning was the Word, and the Word was with God, and the Word was God. He was in the beginning with God. All things were made through Him, and without Him nothing was made that was made. In Him was life, and the life was the light of men . . . And the Word became flesh and dwelt among us, and we beheld His glory.[1]

A work of art speaks a truth we can't speak outright: the truth of the human experience. Love, joy, grief, guilt, beauty—no words can communicate these. We can only represent them in stories and pictures and songs. Art is the way we speak the meaning of our lives.

Throughout the play *Hamlet*, the prince seeks the answer to Pontius Pilate's question: What is truth? How can we tell the difference between our prejudices, our assumptions, our feelings, and the reality around us?

To restate the argument of chapter 2: In the beginning of the play, Hamlet proclaims that his inner world is authentic. His grief for his dead father is beyond mere show. But as the play goes on, he comes to doubt that inner world as a guide to reality. His moods distort his experience of the world. He does not know whether he can act on his own assumptions. He envies those people—an actor, soldiers—who can simply perform their roles in life with complete conviction. At the end of the play, having confronted death, having come to see that "there's a divinity that shapes our ends," he experiences a reversal. He begins to perform life with conviction. He leaps into his dead lover's grave and declares that he can make a show of his grief as well as any man. In the final scene, his entire life becomes a performance. His body is carried to a stage and he becomes the play that has just been put on. Hamlet becomes *Hamlet*. His life becomes a work of art. It becomes the answer to Pilate. It tells the truth he could not find.

Two years before he died, John Keats put it like this: "A Man's life of any worth is a continual allegory, and very few eyes can see the Mystery of his life—a life like the scriptures, figurative."[2]

Our lives are works of art. They speak their meaning.

Jesus' life expresses the Logos, the Word that speaks the world into being, the Word that is with God and that is God. Jesus is that Word made flesh.

The meaning of Jesus' life is the meaning of everything. His truth is truth. His right is right. His beauty is beauty. These are human ideas—truth, right, beauty. These are ways we humans experience the indescribable Logos. But how do we know our truths are true, our right is right, our beauty is beautiful? We know by knowing Jesus. He is what Coleridge said he was: "the World as revealed to human knowledge . . . the total Idea that modifies all thoughts."[3]

When we come to know a person, any person, we come to see at least a little bit of what he sees, to feel and know and experience life along with him. To know Jesus is to experience the Word. "He who puts on the likeness of Christ becomes Christ," Coleridge said.

"Whoever sees me sees him who sent me," said Jesus.[4]

Here's a mental picture of it. Nature is the world in which we live. Meaning is an immaterial realm above nature: the supernatural. As a word—*love*—is language expressing living meaning (the experience of love), so nature—matter, flesh, life—is a language expressing meaning (love, hate, masculine, feminine, good, evil). Language connects nature to meaning. Our flesh is language. Our lives are language. They have a meaning.

We know such connections between nature and meaning exist, and we know that we can get that meaning right or wrong. We know this because of numbers. The next time a scientist tells you all of life is matter, ask him to show you a two. Where is it? What does it look like? How does it taste? He can make a symbol for two: 2. He can show you a two incarnate: two pennies, two bricks.

But two is a human construct of an immaterial truth, a connection in our minds between nature and the truth about nature. We know we can hit or miss that truth because if we use numbers properly, we can predict when light will reach the earth from millions of miles away, and if we use numbers wrongly, we will blow ourselves through the lab window to kingdom come. Numbers connect nature to a truth about nature—or a falsehood—through the mind of man.

Likewise, your life connects nature to the truth of nature, its moral meaning. It is like a number, like a word. To smile at a child or to play the piano speaks something different than to cheat on your spouse or to break a storefront window with a brick. Ultimately, the totality of our lives—our perceptions, words, actions—express the whole idea that is our self, our soul. Your soul is not a ghost in a machine; it is a story your life tells. We are just flesh, but flesh is a language, a word; it speaks of a meaning, right or wrong, good or evil, our selves, our souls.

The prophets knew this. They used their lives as language. They performed their holy visions through actions. Hosea married a prostitute to demonstrate how Israel had gone astray. Jeremiah smashed a jar to show what God would do in his wrath. Ezekiel lay on his side, one side and then the other, for more than a year, eating bread cooked on dung to prophesy about the coming siege of Jerusalem.

John the Baptist did this too. He made himself a literal voice crying in the wilderness to show figuratively that the messianic prophecies of Isaiah were coming to pass. He baptized with water as a metaphor for how the Messiah would baptize with fire and the Holy Spirit.

Jesus goes beyond the prophets. His flesh—his life—his word is the Word. It speaks the structure of meaning, the Logos. He doesn't just perform meaning like Hamlet does or like the prophets do. His life is the meaning. When you lie on your side for a year, that's all meaning, but it's not much of a life. Jesus lives life and everything he does has meaning.

"John came neither eating nor drinking, and they say, 'He has a demon.' The Son of Man came eating and drinking, and they say, 'Here is a glutton and a drunkard, a friend of tax collectors and sinners.' But wisdom is proved right by her deeds," Jesus said.[5]

Jesus lives life, and his life means the Logos. His miracles aren't just metaphors, they're also miracles. When he heals the blind, he tells us he will make us see—but he also heals the blind. When he makes the lame beggar walk, he tells us he will lift our souls out of their crippling deformity—but he also makes the beggar walk. "The works I do in My Father's name testify on My behalf," he said.[6]

He really drinks wine. He really eats with sinners. He loves his friends. He appreciates the beauty of nature, the lilies of the field. He loses his nerve and sweats blood in terror when he faces torture and death. Jesus is meaning, but Jesus is Jesus too, a man in full.

This helps make sense of the things he says and does. Like a great play—like *Hamlet*—everything in his life is both natural and meaningful at the same time.

Peter sees Jesus walking on water. He says, "Lord, if it's you, tell me to come to you." Jesus says, "Come." Peter gets out of the boat and walks on water too. But he becomes afraid and starts to sink.

"Immediately," Scripture says, "Jesus reached out his hand and caught him. 'You of little faith,' he said, 'why did you doubt?'"[7]

But who wouldn't doubt? What man can walk on water? How much faith are we supposed to have?

This is really happening to Peter. He lives it, so that we can understand its meaning. We know that just to live day to day is like walking on water. What we pretend each day is solid ground beneath us is really wavery death capable of swallowing us at any second. We know what it looks like to sink into that element and despair. We know what it's like to move forward by pure denial, never looking down at the truth. But we also know a few, a very few, who walk in full knowledge and full faith, unafraid, eyes on Christ: life in abundance.

Because he is the Word, everything Jesus does is a story, but because he is the Word incarnate, it is also life, because his story is the story of the meaning of life. Picture him as a bridge between the physical world and its immaterial meaning. His life is life, but it is also the truth about life and it is also the way between the two. He is the way and the truth and the life. Take him out of the story and the connection between life and truth is gone; the story becomes meaningless. Which is part of the meaning of his life. Without him, we cannot walk on water, either truly, like Peter, or figuratively, like the rest of us.

And Jesus not only lives the story of life, he tells stories about life. He speaks in parables. "So was fulfilled what was spoken through the prophet: 'I will open my mouth in parables, I will utter things hidden since the creation of the world.'"[8]

Parables don't just convey meaning. The meaning of parables is that they convey meaning. You can't hear them without interpreting them. They force you to confront the fact that meaning exists.

Jesus says, "There was a man who had two sons. The younger one said to his father, 'Father, give me my share of the estate' . . . Not long after that, the younger son . . . set off for a distant country and there squandered his wealth in wild living."[9]

The moment we hear this, we try to connect these natural events to their supernatural meaning. We don't ask ourselves, Which man is Jesus talking about? What were his sons' names? What distant land did the boy go to? We ask instead, What is Jesus telling us here? What is the meaning? What is the truth his parable is trying to convey?

Stories about life have meaning because life has meaning. Parables teach us that we see meaning in life whether or not we believe it's there. The person who says life is meaningless is like Macbeth at the end of the play. Even saying life is meaningless is making meaning out of life: nihilism is a nonsense.

Meaning is above nature—it is supernatural—because it is the idea that nature expresses. This is why Coleridge used the literary supernatural—walking skeletons and the like—in *Rime of the Ancient Mariner* to express the fact that the supernatural Logos is inherent in the natural world. Unbelief in meaning—unbelief in the supernatural—which now seems the sophisticated, intellectual default position, is a nonsense.

When we talk about life as a work of art, a story with a meaning, we're talking about metaphor, a comparison that conveys a truth.

The kingdom of heaven is like a mustard seed. That's a metaphor. At its simplest, the metaphor tells us that the kingdom is a very small thing that can become a very great thing. But, of course, once you start to think about it, the meaning of the metaphor is far vaster and more complex than that. You have to plant a seed, tend it. Once it grows, it attracts more life: the birds in the tree. The meaning goes on and on, deeper and deeper. It's a huge idea. You could think about it forever. If this weren't so, we wouldn't need to use a metaphor. We could simply say the kingdom is a very small thing, but it can become important. That just doesn't do the trick. We need the metaphor to convey and experience the full meaning.

In some sense, all language is metaphor. The word *love* is not love itself; it's a small term we use to describe the vast experience. And since, as *Hamlet* teaches us, our lives are the language of the meaning of our lives, our lives are a metaphor.

A metaphor has three parts: the object we are trying to describe, the term we use to describe it, and the idea that is conveyed when the two come together. In this, a metaphor is itself a metaphor for the Trinity. In the Trinity, the object we are trying to describe is God the Father, the term we use to describe it is Jesus the Son, and when we grasp that idea, we are filled with the Spirit.

The Trinity is a fractal: it is the pattern of all creation that is repeated in every aspect of creation. Everywhere, in everything, there is always the object, the term, and the meaning.

Metaphor is even built into the basic structure of creation. DNA is a code. A code is a kind of language. DNA expresses an idea—the idea of a man and a woman together—and brings it into being as you or me.

And what is that new person? In his book *The Consciousness*

Instinct, Michael S. Gazzaniga, one of the leading experts on the human mind, says metaphor is built into human consciousness too. What human consciousness is, he says, is an instinct for creating symbols to represent experience to ourselves.[10]

Human consciousness is the ability to create metaphors for reality.

Creation is a fractal: it is metaphors all the way down. The three-part Logos creates man, man creates metaphors for reality, reality is a metaphor for the Logos.

Jesus, the Word made flesh, is the flesh that speaks the Word, our guide to when our metaphors tell the truth about reality and when they do not. Led by what Coleridge called "the total Idea that modifies all thoughts," each of us is, as Wordsworth said, "an agent of the one great mind . . . creator and receiver both, working but in alliance with the works which it beholds."

Each of us learns to do this, Wordsworth said, in his first experience of love, when his soul "drinks in the feelings of his Mother's eye!"[11]

For the Word to become flesh, for the Logos to become fully human, even God needs a mother.

2. BORN OF A VIRGIN: JESUS, HUMANITY, AND THE ETERNAL FEMININE

God sent the angel Gabriel to Nazareth, a town in Galilee, to a virgin pledged to be married to a man named Joseph, a descendant of David. The virgin's name was Mary . . . The

> angel said to her . . . "You will conceive and give birth to a son, and you are to call him Jesus." . . .
>
> "How will this be," Mary asked the angel, "since I am a virgin?"
>
> The angel answered, "The Holy Spirit will come on you, and the power of the Most High will overshadow you. So the holy one to be born will be called the Son of God."[12]

When I reread the Gospels to try to get to know Jesus, I did my best to read them as if for the first time. "Maybe you are trying to understand a philosophy instead of trying to get to know a man," my son had said to me. So I taught myself Greek and read the four books as I would read a novel or a biography, trying to let the characters, especially the main character, come to life in my mind.

I approached the books as if they were what the evangelist Luke said they were: "An account of the things that have been fulfilled among us, just as they were handed down to us by those who from the first were eyewitnesses and servants of the word."[13]

I treated the texts as "God-breathed" or inspired, but not as magic. These are the works of real men writing about real events as they were witnessed or passed down. It would strike me as suspiciously inauthentic if each evangelist did not see Jesus in a different way. What two people give exactly the same accounts of a third person? That never happens, never. The more different accounts we receive about someone, the more we understand him in the round.

Finally, I tried to come to these accounts fresh, without theology, without piety, without tradition, without prejudice. I tried to set aside even my own opinions. If what follows, then, is different in some places from what many believers know for certain to be true, it's because I came to the four witnesses as a fifth witness, to see and know the man for myself.

I did not find Mary to be the Holy Mother of Catholic tradition. A perennial virgin conceived immaculately without original sin, able to give birth without a pang, assumed bodily into heaven—that isn't what I read about her in the texts. I think maybe this is instead an image of perfected femininity—what Goethe called the Eternal Feminine. "The Eternal Feminine leads us on," he said.[14] Maybe Mary suggests this image to us because she is the mother of the Logos. Her life expresses the feminine as Jesus expresses the Word.

This makes sense to me, profound sense. Giving birth to God by God does seem to me to be the ultimate feminine act and the ultimate human act as well. I sometimes hear feminists complain that God should not be represented only as male—as Father—because God contains both masculine and feminine. And of course, it's true: we know God contains both masculine and feminine because he made both men and women in his image. But God is always male to us because we are always female to him, the bride to his bridegroom. We bring out of ourselves what he puts into us. So in giving birth to Jesus, Mary is not just femininity incarnate, she is humanity incarnate, humanity in its relationship with God.

But—and again, this is just my reading of the texts—Mary lived out the Eternal Feminine just as other women live it out, in the life of a flesh-and-blood woman. After conceiving Jesus miraculously, she was married to Joseph. We know Joseph was alive at least twelve years after Jesus' birth. We know that Jesus had brothers and sisters. So I assume that Mary's body was made as other women's: to take mankind into itself with pleasure and bring mankind out of itself in pain.

In living the life of a woman of her time, Mary was like all women. But in giving birth to the Logos and nurturing him into full humanity, she was the feminine in the flesh.

And Jesus was fully human too. He couldn't have done what he did unless he was. "No one has ever seen God," said John, "but the one and only Son, who is himself God and is in closest relationship with the Father, has made him known."[15]

Still, in being flesh and blood, Jesus was distinct from God the Father. He did not know everything the Father knows—when the end of time would come, for instance. His will, contained in flesh, was distinct from the Father's will. "Not my will be done," he prayed when he was facing death, "but yours."[16] The Father cannot die. The Father does not fear. Jesus could and did.

The Father lives in the realm of meaning, out of time. There is no time when he does not know all things. But in time, Jesus is the moment when God learns the one thing an eternal, omniscient being can't otherwise know: mortality, the limits of the flesh, the limits of human insight and knowledge, the experience of our tragic brokenness. Jesus learns to know himself as a man as all men must, in stages. And Mary, like every mother, was an essential part of that learning, a foil and fellow traveler.

Jesus understood when very young that he was the Son of God, or at least a son of God. He possessed a cold, clear certainty he had a mission that surpassed all other earthly obligations.

When he was twelve, he went missing. After celebrating the Passover in Jerusalem with his family, he did not join the caravan heading home. At first, no one noticed. Then, after a day's journey, his parents realized their eldest son was not with them. They headed back to the city, desperately searching for him.

They found him finally in the temple. He was speaking with the rabbis there, astonishing everyone with his wisdom.

Mary said exactly what you would expect her to say: "Son, why have You done this to us? Look, Your father and I have sought You anxiously."

Jesus answered, "Why did you seek Me? Did you not know that I must be about My Father's business?"[17]

His parents did not understand his answer. How could they? Who would? "Why did you seek me?" It was a ferocious thing to say, a ferocious thing to do, an act of ferocious self-certainty, ferocious and self-certain as only an adolescent can be, superior and indifferent to the fear and suffering his disappearance must have caused his parents. Why did they seek him? How could he ask?

Jesus knew early on who he was, but he did not know, he could not know, who we are, how small, how broken, how frightened we are, what he would have to do on our behalf.

He retained his certainty and purpose throughout his life. He was always wandering off to preach or pray, leaving his followers to search for him, to catch up. But over time, the ferocity became tinted with humility and compassion as he witnessed and experienced what a limited and tragic thing it is to be what we are. He dined with sinners. He upbraided religious leaders for the sake of the people. He worked to make us understand what he saw. Over time, he began to realize that we could not see it as easily he did. Many could not see it at all.

When he came to John by the Jordan, he clearly accepted the Baptist as a mentor. They were both aware from the start he was the student who would surpass the teacher. "I need to be baptized by you," John said, "and do you come to me?" But there was still a learning experience that had to be gone through. "It is proper for us to do this to fulfill all righteousness," Jesus replied.[18] I don't think this was just a matter of form. It was part of becoming human, which is a process that occurs in time. We don't become people by ourselves. We don't become people right away. A baby needs to look into his mother's eyes to learn humanity. A boy needs a father or a father figure to become a man.

When John was arrested, Jesus set about preaching on his own. But for a while, he seems to have continued to spread John's message. He baptized people. He called them to repentance—to *metanoia*, a change of mind.

It was after John's execution that Jesus stepped out before the Baptist's shattered followers and took his place at the head of the movement. It was then he refashioned the movement to fit his increasing understanding of what it meant to be himself in the mortal world of women and men.

I think the transfiguration marks the fullness of that understanding, the completion of the revelation of what it meant to be the Son of the Father on earth. Jesus took Peter and two other disciples into a high mountain. There, he was transformed before them. "His face shone like the sun, and his clothes became as white as the light."[19] Elijah appeared on one side of him, Moses on the other: he was the fulfillment of Jewish prophecy and Jewish law; his life was the recapitulation of God's revelation of himself through Jewish history. He was that history made individual, the Word made flesh.

Out of the bright cloud that covered them, God spoke aloud. "This is my Son, whom I love," he said.

It was around this time—as this time approached and just afterward—that Jesus came to realize what would be required of him. This was when he began to speak of how he would have to suffer and die. Not because of who he was. Because of who we are.

Through all this, Mary was also learning these things. Trying to understand them. Suffering in her growing knowledge as any mother would. She had been told by an angel that she would be made pregnant by the Holy Spirit. She had witnessed wonders and stored them in her heart. She worked to comprehend the extraordinary eldest child who, by the rules of normal life, should never have been inside her in the first place.

But normal life and its normal rules lay a powerful veil over the supernatural. They do for all of us. Even those who have witnessed miracles stop fully believing in them over time as the nonmiraculous day-by-day works its way on their consciousness.

What sense could this peasant mother make of the wild things she'd seen and heard? How could any mother face the full consequences of them?

I know I'm playing with some of the traditional timelines and redacting here and there, but when I read the events of Jesus' ministry, I see a natural progression in the relationship between mother and son.

Jesus was rejected in Nazareth. But the crowds of Galilee continued to gather around him because of the wonders he performed. His mother and brothers came out to find him. He was making amazing claims about himself. They were afraid he might have gone insane. They tried to get to him, through the crowds, but Jesus, still ferocious, wouldn't let them come. He had to establish he was who he was. He had to do what he had to do.

When told his mother and brothers were waiting to see him, he responded, "Who are my mother and brothers?" Then he pointed to his disciples and said, "Here are my mother and my brothers. For whoever does the will of my Father in heaven is my brother and sister and mother."[20]

To me, these sound like the words of a man fiercely declaring his remarkable stature in the midst of those who knew him as a child. The people of Nazareth asked themselves, "Isn't this the carpenter's son? Isn't his mother's name Mary, and aren't his brothers James, Joseph, Simon and Judas?"[21] We saw this kid grow up. How miraculous can he be?

His family must have felt the same way. His mother and brothers and sisters. They knew him as a baby, as a boy, as a brother, as a son. How miraculous could he be? Maybe he'd just gone out of his mind.

I know that the wedding at Cana where Jesus turned the water to wine is supposed to be the first of his miracles. But I can't help but wonder whether the scene represents a slightly later moment, the moment when Mary, having stored so much that was unbelievable in her heart, finally began to believe, to fully accept the truth about her son, and the moment when he began to relax with her in the knowledge that she would accept his need to do the uncompromising, dangerous, maybe fatal work he had to do.

In *The Last Temptation of Christ*, a daring novelistic retelling of the Gospels, author Nikos Kazantzakis catches this all-too-human mother-and-son dynamic. He has Mary react in horror when a rabbi suggests to her that Jesus may be a prophet:

"Have pity on me, Father!" she cries. "A prophet? No, no! . . . I want my son a man like everyone else, nothing more, nothing less."

"If God listened to mothers," the rabbi responds severely, "we would all rot away in a bog of security and easy living."[22]

That is the last temptation of the title: Jesus' temptation to live out his mother's wish for him—a normal life. He is tempted to marry, to love, to be "a man like everyone else, nothing more, nothing less."

A man who breaks away from his mother to do the extraordinary is breaking away from himself as well: from her nurturing, which in making him becomes the heart of him; from her maternal fears, which in protecting him become inner limits he has to overcome; from her griefs, which, in his love for her, are his griefs as well. His struggle to become an individual is all the more fierce because that individuality was a gift that flowed from her to him both physically and spiritually. Even after he cuts the umbilicus, the omphalos will always be his core.

At first, the exchange between Mary and Jesus at the Cana wedding read strangely to me. It read harshly. She points out to him that the wedding hosts are running out of wine. This would be a social calamity for the hosts. It would disgrace them. Jesus knows she is asking him to perform a miracle.

"Woman," he says severely, "what have I to do with thee? Mine hour is not yet come."[23]

Without another word, Mary turns to the servants. She tells

them to do whatever Jesus instructs them: to fill the wine jugs with water, to prepare for the miracle he is about to perform.

Then Jesus turns the water into wine, just as she wanted.

I see this as the moment when mother and son came to understand and accept one another. In asking him for a miracle, Mary accepted who Jesus was as a man, the unbelievable truth about him that had haunted her since the annunciation. And Jesus accepted that, well, even when you're a man, your mother is still your mother. She asked for a miracle with an authority over him she could no longer have. He rebuked her. She showed that, all the same, she expected him to do what she asked, if not on command than in filial love. He did what she asked.

It's really rather beautiful when you read it that way. After his ferocious youth—when he was willing to walk away from his parents to do his father's business—he softens here because he realizes that Mary has now fully affirmed his vision of himself and his right to act independently. She has shown she knows the truth about his miraculous powers. He has not gone mad. He really is who he says he is.

In coming to understand that, Mary must have also begun to understand, must at least have suspected, that she was now committed to his whole mission, committed even to standing at the foot of the cross and watching her firstborn die in agony—an incomprehensible grief for a mother, a heartbreaking act of maternal faith and womanly devotion.

"He for God only. She for God in him."[24]

What John Milton wrote of Adam and Eve—and, by extension, of men and women in general—was true of Mary and Jesus: he was for God only, and she was for God in him.

In our egalitarian age, such a hierarchy startles us, as C. S. Lewis said. Some of us are repelled by it. But the early Christians clearly saw this dynamic at the heart of the feminine-masculine divide. It is the source of the guidance in Ephesians that some now find controversial: "Wives, submit yourselves to your own husbands as you do to the Lord . . . Husbands, love your wives, just as Christ loved the church."[25]

Essentially, this is an instruction for us to perform our femininity and masculinity as a means of expressing the Logos with our lives, to use our bodies as the language of holy meaning, the flesh made Word. Woman, become womanhood, which is humanity in its relationship with God. Man, become manhood, which is a metaphor for Christ. He for God only. She for God in him.

To give your life over to such spiritual meanings is an affront to the material world and is sure to incur the world's hostility. The marketplace does not want to lose its women workers to the nursery. The state does not want to cede its power to the fathers of families. In material terms, it's unfair; it's oppressive. So the world is sure to turn its science and technology and social systems to "solving the problem" of gender, which is really just the problem of femininity and its core in spiritual action. The world will learn to grow babies in machines, to nurture them in institutions, to free women for the market, to strip men of their authority, to make us the same.

And who knows? Maybe that's for the best. To live into the meaning of our genders is perhaps to sacrifice a great deal that is good in the world. Dedicated homemakers lose career advancement and prestige. Dedicated husbands sacrifice the pleasures of irresponsibility and promiscuity. There were good reasons radicals like Mary Shelley's father and mother and husband derided marriage and felt there had to be a better way.

But if Coleridge was right, and humanity and nature are one creation; if Wordsworth was right, and we find our humanity at our mother's breast; then Mary Shelley was also right, and if we "solve" our natures with science, we might end up "solving" our humanity entirely. And women—women-as-women—will be the first thing to go.

I have no interest in declaring how people should organize their personal lives. Jesus said, "Judge not,"[26] and I take that to heart: if you are peering into another person's soul, you are looking in the wrong direction. But after a long life, I can report anecdotally that all the most joyful people I have ever met were married, and all the happiest marriages I have ever seen were arranged, in some sense, on the Ephesian principles. Like many spiritual endeavors, such marriages seem to the materialist mind like they should be unfair and oppressive, but in actuality, they're not. They're the very opposite.

Perhaps my observations are limited to my social set or my culture or my time. But it also seems at least possible to me that when we lose our lives for the sake of the Word made flesh, we find our lives in a much deeper way—maybe even an eternal way—as the flesh made Word.

Each of us, of course, must choose freely for himself or herself. Those who have ears to hear, let them hear.

3. BELIEVE THE WORKS: JESUS VERSUS SCIENTIFIC MATERIALISM

When the sun was setting, all those who had any that were sick with various diseases brought them to Him; and He laid His hands on every one of them and healed them.[27]

I used to know a woman who had dated a famous faith healer. She told me once that he had healed a man with a shortened leg. She said he put his hands on the man and made the short leg grow so that it was the same length as the other.

"No, he didn't," I said.

"I saw him," she said.

"No," I said. "You didn't."

I didn't believe it then. I don't believe it now. I have never heard of a famous faith healer who was not eventually exposed as a fraud. The man she dated eventually was as well.

But to be a Christian, we have to believe in the healings and miracles of Jesus. He cites them as proof of his identity. When John the Baptist is in prison, he sends his followers to ask if Jesus is the Messiah. Jesus responds, "Go back and report to John what you have seen and heard: The blind receive sight, the lame walk, those who have leprosy are cleansed, the deaf hear, the dead are raised, and the good news is proclaimed to the poor."[28]

"The works I do in My Father's name testify about Me," he says elsewhere. "Even though you do not believe Me, believe the works, that you may know and understand that the Father is in Me, and I in Him."[29]

The miracles can't be explained away.

I don't actually struggle very much with doubt. I did not become a Christian until I was forty-nine, so I had a lot of time to think things through. I'm pretty sure I got it right and that Jesus is who he says he is. But when doubts do cavil at me, it's always about this—about the miracles. Our scientific understanding of the world has given us a deep instinctive sense that the miraculous is simply not how the world works. You can't chase lightning away by ringing church bells.

And of course, we all believe that, the faithful and the faith-less both. We all believe that the world doesn't normally work in a miraculous way. If it did, if everyone went about healing people all the time, Jesus would not have cited his works as special evidence of who he was.

So atheists don't believe in God because miracles don't happen. And Christians do believe in him because miracles don't happen— then they did.

There aren't many miracles in the Old Testament. Depending on how you count them, I'd estimate there's somewhere around a hundred of them spread out over thousands and thousands of years. A large portion of them are clustered around the period of the exodus.

And we have to remember, as C. S. Lewis points out, that every miracle has a reasonable explanation after it happens. It's only before it happens that it's impossible. So miracles leave no traces of themselves except the testimony of witnesses.

I myself have seen several miracles in my life. Really, I don't believe the dramatic and complete healing of my early mental illness would have occurred without the direct intervention of God. I've never seen anything else like it anywhere. I've never even heard of anything like it. So a hundred extraordinary occurrences between the creation and the Jewish return from the Babylonian exile is not all that incredible a tally to me.

Still, when Jesus comes on the scene, everything changes. When he's around, the miraculous becomes commonplace. Matthew tells us Jesus "went throughout Galilee . . . healing every disease and sickness among the people."[30] That's probably a bit of artistic hyperbole. Hyperbole seems to be the only way to communicate what happened. If every work Jesus performed were recorded, John says, "I suppose that the world itself could not contain the books that would be written."[31] That's a lot of miracles.

In his time, when there were living witnesses, Jesus could cite the miracles as reason to believe in who he was. But now, long after, in this scientific age, with all the witnesses dead and gone, our belief in who he was is our reason to believe in the miracles.

What is it we doubt when we doubt them? We think we doubt that such things could ever happen at all, but I don't believe that's correct.

Try a mind experiment.

What if one day someone strolling about the Middle East stumbled on a buried spaceship—tripped over it, like the heroine in Stephen King's horror novel *The Tommyknockers*? The thing is dug up and scientists determine it's an alien craft that was buried here on earth around two thousand years ago. Within the vehicle, they discover flexible metallic material of a type that simply doesn't exist on this planet: more proof this is an intergalactic relic.

There are markings on the material. They look like a form of space writing. Great minds go to work with high-tech software and soon they have translated the writing into English.

"I, EkTok-12," the text begins, "on the eve of my return to my home planet via teleportation, here record this narrative of my sojourn on Earth, where I was known as Jesus of Nazareth."

EkTok-12, aka Jesus, then proceeds to describe how he performed the miracles pretty much as we have them in the Gospels.

Would we believe the miracles happened then?

I think we would, easily. Given the proper proofs that this was truly the souvenir of a visit by a superior race from outer space, I think only the knee-jerk skeptics would cling to their doubts.

It's not the miracles we don't believe in, it's the source of the miracles. It's the immaterial God of creation we cannot allow into our material mindset.

.

Every instinct tells us that at the height of its power, the human mind can control matter. Stories of gods, stories of magic, stories of science fiction—though perhaps with less ridiculous character names than EkTok-12—all speak of our belief in the possibility. Whenever we imagine the human mind expanded to the limits of enlightenment—in movies like *Star Wars*, *Phenomenon*, or *Doctor Strange*—we portray that enlightenment in terms of the mind controlling matter, even to the point of manipulating space and time.

What's more, as scientific discovery progresses, the possibility of such mind-power begins to appear on the far horizon of reality. We've already begun to communicate directly with computers. We can write on them merely by thinking, play games and make mechanical robots walk around the room all through our thoughts. So far, this requires some kind of brain-computer interface, some physical connection to transfer the electrical impulses in our brains to the machines. But at the quantum level of matter, we have already found the sort of "spooky action at a distance" that Einstein said was impossible—objects affecting each other without any apparent physical connection at all—so physical connections may not always be necessary.[32] What's more, scientists have found objects at this quantum level whose nature and location are only statistical possibilities—until we view them or measure them, then suddenly the possibilities collapse, and they exist in a specific way in a specific place. It looks very much as if consciousness has a role in the creation of the physical world.

Which is, of course, the first assertion of religious faith—that consciousness, acting at a distance, has a role in creation, that consciousness precedes creation, that it is creation's source and motive force and can bring what was not there into existence and change what is there into something new. This is the very first thing that happens in the Bible. God says let there be light—and there is. And it's what Jesus does in the miracles and healings. He uses consciousness to affect matter.

Those scientists who embrace materialism refuse to believe in the creative role of consciousness. They are so committed to the idea that it can't exist that they have begun inventing outlandish and unproveable theories to explain away what they perceive with their own formulas and instruments. They imagine infinite indemonstrable universes that cause the effects they witness, or they speculate that we are living in some sort of computer-generated simulation. The same people who wax eloquent about Occam's razor—the theory that the simplest explanation is probably the right one—are willing to believe that a giant invisible geek with a magic computer is inventing the universe as an experiment rather than concede the slightest credence to the white-bearded Jew on the ceiling of the Sistine Chapel who thought life into Adam and all the world.

Religious people used to be chided for inventing a "God of the gaps," a God who provides supernatural explanations for whatever science has not yet explained. That's fair enough. But there is now a science of the gaps, in which materialists scramble to come up with wilder and wilder notions to explain away the creative power of consciousness and the mind-matter interface that is at the heart of faith.

And yet everywhere that interface—at least the possibility of that interface—keeps emerging. The odds against creation; the connection between man-made mathematics and the invisible structures of experience; the virtual impossibility of even the simplest living cell ever coming to be—all this tells us, in the words of the famously atheist scientist Fred Hoyle, that "a superintellect has monkeyed with physics, as well as with chemistry and biology."[33] It seems more and more likely that the message of the burning bush to Moses was right: nature, this great machine of material creation and destruction, is the spoken word of a consciousness that is crying out to us, "I AM THAT I AM."[34]

Personally, I suspect scientific atheism is a holdover from another time, a once-reasonable idea that has become obsolete. After Newton began to explain the physical workings of the world, it may have made sense for people to extrapolate from his theories to a wholly mechanical clockwork universe—although Newton himself never believed in that at all. But things have not turned out the way we expected them to. They are much, much weirder.

At this point, I think it is actually more plausible to believe that matter is the spoken word of the One Great Mind than that it is simply itself. Mathematics would not work if this were not so—it would have no underlying idea to which to refer. Truth, morality, and beauty likewise—they would be smoke and illusion, as the materialists say they are.

But they're not. Math, truth, morality, and beauty are all ways in which our minds translate matter into meaning—the Logos—the meaning in the consciousness of the Great Mind.

And since our minds are made in the Great Mind's image, there is no reason not to believe that his Word could appear among us in the guise of ourselves. Like all miracles, it seems unlikely only before it happens. Afterward, it seems entirely reasonable.

Such a person, the embodied Word, would be the clear mirror which shows us the image of moral reality we now see only darkly. He would be the silent presence of the truth the language of our lives can only roughly express. And he would be inexpressible except as presence, as story, as a living metaphor for himself. He would be like the experience of bread and wine—indescribable. You have to taste and see that it's good.

To such a person—to the Word made flesh—the incidentals of material existence, the things we worry about most—our health, our money, our power, our lives—would be mere allegory, their brokenness fixable in a finger-snap. His existence would be what material existence is about. His mind would be one with the web of being. Miracles, healings, walking on water—he could do it all— all the things our instincts and our stories tell us we ourselves might one day do.

"Whoever believes in me," he might promise us, "will do the works I have been doing, and they will do even greater things than these."[35]

Because that promise has not yet come true—because famous faith healers turn out to be frauds—theologians reach for metaphorical interpretations. What Jesus meant by that promise, they say, is this: as he gave signs that point to God, so we also may give such signs.

But I see it rather as a long-term pledge to the "body of Christ," a forecast that, by following him, we will create a science that is not dehumanizing, not the way science can now often be, not a Frankensteinian conquest of nature which can end only by being the conquest of ourselves, but the full humanization of nature as the language of the Logos, as a path to a truly moral existence, in which we too, like little Jesuses, are interwoven with the understructure of matter in a new heaven and a new earth where all that is broken is made whole. Jesus often tells the people he heals, "Your faith has made you well."[36] It is as if his healing is not a power coming out of him but an alignment of our minds with his. What could we not accomplish when so aligned?

Twice, Jesus heals blind men by putting his spit in their eyes. Once, in Galilee, he mixes his saliva with dirt and uses the resultant mud as a salve. Science reduces all things to mere matter. But all the matter that Jesus perceives becomes holy, an expression of the spirit-consciousness that created it. His science is not reductive. It melds the world with the Logos, the moral meaning of which he is the incarnation.

The other blind man Jesus meets, in Jerusalem, doesn't heal fully on the first application of saliva. He starts to see the men around him, but he says, "They look like trees walking around."[37] Only on the second try does Jesus bring him to see the men in their full humanity. Not trees but people, the possessor of the consciousness that makes trees what they are, the mind that cocreates them with the One Great Mind, that names them, that hears the noise when they fall and therefore brings it into being: crash.

In these miracles—which are, like everything he does, both an action and a parable—he seems to be calling on us to heal the blindness that resulted from our original sin, to see again what we might once have seen in Eden: that we are the soul of nature and nature is the language of the One Great Soul.

Jesus sometimes seems perplexed by our inability to see what he sees and to do the amazing things he does. The possibilities are so obvious to him, he is frustrated that we are so blind. "O ye of little faith," he says when Peter can't walk on water.[38] "You unbelieving and perverse generation," he says when the disciples can't cast out a demon that is torturing a child. "How long shall I stay with you? How long shall I put up with you?"[39]

The full truth—the Logos—is right there in front of us. It's so clear, how can we miss it?

This is the one thing the living Logos could not possibly know: what it is like to be fallen away from the Logos. What it is like to live in sin. What it is like to be us.

I wonder if this is why Jesus weeps when he sees the people mourning for the dead Lazarus. I can't make any other sense of it.

He has been told that Lazarus, his friend, is ill. Yet he delays going to him so that the man dies before he gets there.

"I am glad I was not there, so that you may believe," he says. He is going to lift him out of death to demonstrate that even death is nothing when we see as Jesus sees.[40]

By the time the Christ arrives in Bethany, where Lazarus lived, the man has been dead for four days. Lazarus's sister, Jesus' friend, Martha, a practical housewife, warns him not to roll away the stone because her brother will have begun to stink. The corpse is already decaying so that there is now absolutely no chance the man can be revived.

Jesus clearly makes a show of his most spectacular miracle. Like everything he does, it is both itself and a performance of itself. He even calls out to God "for the benefit of the people standing here, that they may believe that you sent me."[41] What he wants them to know is not that he *can* do this, but that he *is* this, the Word made flesh, which is the resurrection and the life. He is going to enormous lengths to make sure people get the point.

But then Martha's sister, Mary, approaches with the other locals. She is sobbing with grief. They all are. Jesus knows the grief is unnecessary. He knows he is about to demonstrate beyond a shadow of doubt that death is as nothing in the kingdom of heaven. So why, then, knowing that, does he see the mourners and become "deeply moved in spirit and troubled"?[42]

Well, it was one thing for Martha not to wholly understand who he is. She's a down-to-earth homemaker, a *balaboosta*, who takes care of the business of this world. But Mary is the mystic sister. She's the one who stops everything whenever Jesus comes to visit them. She sits at his feet and listens to his preaching, womanly wise. If anyone should understand him by now, she's the one.

So maybe this is where Jesus is struck fully and finally with just how very, very blind we are, how tragic in our lack of understanding, how deeply immersed in sin. Even in the very presence of the resurrection, we can't fully grasp or believe in it. He says he has spoken to us "that my joy may be in you, and that your joy may be full."[43] But we have no joy. The world is too much with us late and soon, and the world, to us, is all fear and all mourning all the time.

Which only confirms what he has already prophesied: this is his death warrant; he must die to take us where we need to go. And even then, for some, it will not matter. For those of us who haven't already learned the nature of the Logos from Moses and the prophets, "neither will they be convinced if someone should rise from the dead."[44]

Seeing this, Jesus wept. For us.

4. THE KINGDOM OF HEAVEN: JESUS VERSUS RADICAL POLITICS

Once, on being asked by the Pharisees when the kingdom of God would come, Jesus replied, "The coming of the kingdom of God is not something that can be observed, nor will people say, 'Here it is,' or 'There it is,' because the kingdom of God is in your midst."[45]

There was a time in the distant past when the people of Israel lived without rulers, "and every man did that which was right in his own eyes."[46] They had the prophets then to advise them of the will of God, and military leaders who rose up to deal with emergencies.

But when the prophets became corrupt, the people demanded to have a king, "such as all the other nations have." The prophet Samuel warned them what governments do: how they make servants of the people and tax the best of their goods for their own purposes. But God told Samuel, "It is not you they have rejected, but they have rejected me as their king." So Samuel gave in and gave Israel the king they asked for.[47]

To me, it seems like a second fall from a second Eden. They

strayed away from freedom and stepped into the cycle of history: to government and King David's empire and the fall of that empire, the inevitable fate of all empires.

Jesus came to a conquered people. Their country was a client state of Rome. A proud and fiercely religious race, who believed themselves the chosen of God, they were suffering the daily humiliation of occupation. Their priests were corrupted by compromise with their pagan overlords. Radicals, inspired by the successful Maccabean revolt against the Seleucid Empire only a century and a half before, were committing terrorist attacks, hoping to stir a rebellion. They had no idea what they were up against. The Romans were not the Seleucids. When they lost their patience with the rebels around 70 AD, they wiped the Jewish nation off the face of the earth like brushing away a fly.

It's no wonder the Jews were looking for a son of King David to lead them back to the days of their imperial greatness. Instead, they got a messiah who wanted to lead them back to the days before those days, the days of true freedom under God's rule. Render unto Caesar that which is Caesar's, he told them, unto God that which is God's.[48]

His kingdom was not of this world.

To live into the meaning of life—to live, as Keats said, as "a continual allegory . . . a life like the scriptures, figurative," to live as if the flesh were a parable of the spirit—is to live in the kingdom of heaven while on earth.[49]

The kingdom of heaven is a small thing, but it is everything. It is the "least of all the seeds"[50] that a man plants, and yet it grows into a mighty tree in which the birds can live. It is like the pinch of yeast that a woman puts in a large batch of dough so that the whole thing rises. It's like the tiny pearl that is so valuable a merchant sells everything he owns to possess it.

But what does it look like in action?

Jesus was teaching in the temple when "the scribes and the Pharisees brought a woman who had been caught in adultery; and making her stand before all of them, they said to him, 'Teacher, this woman was caught in the very act of committing adultery. The law of Moses commanded us to stone such women. Now what do you say?' They said this to test him, so that they might have some charge to bring against him. Jesus bent down and wrote with his finger on the ground. When they kept on questioning him, he straightened up and said to them, 'Let anyone among you who is without sin be the first to throw a stone at her.' And once again he bent down and wrote on the ground. When they heard it, they went away, one by one, beginning with the elders; and Jesus was left alone with the woman standing before him. Jesus straightened up and said to her, 'Woman, where are they? Has no one condemned you?' She said, 'No one, sir.' And Jesus said, 'Neither do I condemn you; go and sin no more.'"[51]

It is easy to imagine what the inhabitants of our current political categories would make of this event if they had been on the scene. The radicals would demand to know why Jesus did not denounce this brutally cruel law. Death by stoning for an adulteress? What an outrage. The conservatives would say, "Yes, but if we don't stone her, then *everyone* will commit adultery."

No political thinker likes this story, not really, not as it stands. There was even a movement among some conservatives recently to have the story removed from the Gospels as inauthentic. Since the incident doesn't appear in the earliest gospel manuscripts, they said, it may have been added later by unscrupulous copyists.

But there are traces of the story in very early traditions. And to my mind, if anything in the New Testament sounds like Jesus talking, it's this. My guess is that the story of Jesus and the adulteress was edited out of the first manuscripts because its implications are so incredibly problematic for anyone who thinks mere law can solve the human condition.

Yet religious conservatives, too, who are committed to the idea of the inerrant integrity of Scripture, will go a long way to interpret the obvious meaning out of this passage. They speculate about what Jesus was writing on the ground. Perhaps it was some verse from Leviticus that exposed the hypocrisy of the accusers. They take the same approach to Christ's injunction, "Judge not, lest you be judged."[52] He meant, "Do not judge hypocritically," they say. In general, they are in a big hurry to skate over all this not-judging funny business and proceed directly to the bit about "go and sin no more," which, to be sure, is an excellent idea.

But no. To see this incident as a rebuke to mere hypocrisy is to overlook the core of the moment, the most startling words in the passage, Jesus' words to the adulteress after the mob fails to condemn her: "Neither do I condemn you." Since he has invited anyone who is without sin to throw the first stone, and since he is without sin, he could've gotten the whole hit-the-girl-with-rocks party started himself. But he didn't. The Son of God gave her a pass for what was then, and is now, a violation of one of God's central commandments. Hypocrisy was not the issue. Judgment was. And he did not judge her.

On the other hand, no radical could be satisfied with this

scenario either. It is hard for a modern person to believe it was ever a good idea—that it was ever an expression of God's justice—to execute people for adultery, or to execute anyone by throwing rocks at them until they were dead. And yet this was what the law of Moses demanded. How barbaric!

Jesus was not afraid to address such issues. When he was asked about the Mosaic law allowing men to divorce their wives—a law that left women in a pitiably vulnerable position—he said Moses gave the people that law because of the hardness of their hearts. "But it was not this way from the beginning," he said, when marriage made a man and woman "one flesh"[53] that could not be torn asunder by human means. I don't think we fully appreciate how shocking a revision to the sacred texts this was, what a new and powerful protection for women. The men in the audience were appalled.

Yet in the case of the adulteress, Jesus leaves the bloody law intact. He doesn't denounce it. He doesn't crusade for "social justice," whatever that might mean. He does not make the error of radicals that Edmund Burke described: cutting away the tradition that shaped the very moral structure of the people to whom he's speaking. The culture that caused them to drop their stones was created by the tradition that commanded them to pick them up in the first place. The law was given to them to ready their hard hearts to receive the underlying principle of the law.

So with the law on adultery, just as he did with the law on divorce, Jesus returns to the origins of the tradition, the tradition on which the tradition stands. "Thou shalt love the Lord thy God with all thy heart, and with all thy soul, and with all thy mind. This is the first and great commandment. And the second is like unto it, Thou shalt love thy neighbour as thyself. On these two commandments hang all the law and the prophets," Jesus said.[54]

Holding the accusers to these principles, he then leaves them free to enforce the penalty or not. They don't—and neither does he.

He does not need to rewrite the law of Moses. He infuses the law with the love in which the law was given. And by some wonder beyond the power of mere justice, the law erases itself with its own hand.

Matter is the language of the Logos. Our lives are meant to express the truth and beauty which is woven into the fabric of God's creation. But like all languages, matter is a rude tool that cannot wholly express, but can only hint at, the silent fullness of reality. There are always gaps between the truth of things and our expression of the truth. There are grey areas between a word and its meaning. In the case of moral life, there are ethical questions that can't be solved by reason or the law. Do you torture a man to prevent a terrorist attack? Do you allow a train to hit five people by accident or divert it to kill one person on purpose? Do you confess a past adultery and destroy your family, or do you keep your marriage intact and live a lie? Ethicists debate such questions endlessly, but they can't quite force the language of matter and moral truth into perfect harmony. No one can.

Every day, in hospitals around the country, probably around the world, doctors kill patients who are beyond all hope. I have seen this done with my own eyes. They say, "We will increase the dosage of morphine each hour to keep him comfortable." What they mean is, "We have done everything we can and now we will put him out of his misery."

In places where the laws against euthanasia are removed, unforgiveable exterminations become acceptable—as when a depressed seventeen-year-old girl was recently euthanized in the Netherlands, an act of certain evil. And yet in places where the laws are enforced too strictly, unbearable suffering is prolonged unnecessarily. The truth is, the law can't cover every moral situation. We sometimes have to act in the shadows, prayerfully groping toward the good of an individual case in order to give "measure for measure," as Shakespeare says in his play on the subject.[55]

The very presence of law—without which we cannot live as civilized people—is in conflict with the presence of virtue. Virtue—goodness—can only be chosen freely. If it is not chosen, it is not truly good. If I point a gun at you and order you to give money to charity, that does not make you charitable. It just means you're afraid to die. To do good, and therefore to be good, you must be free of constraint and yet freely allow yourself to be ruled by God—like the Israelites before they had a king.

If each person can't act freely according to his conscience, there can be no virtue. But if each person's conscience isn't governed by the Word of God, a lawless land is full of chaos, brutality, and corruption, might over right. We need the law to live, but the law, like government itself, feeds on its own reasoning and grows and grows until it destroys not only the opportunity for virtue but virtue itself. If Jesus often battled the Pharisees over the letter of the Mosaic law, this was why. "The letter killeth," as Paul famously wrote, "but the spirit giveth life."[56]

The problem put simply is this: we feel certain there is a sphere of perfect moral meaning, but we can see that this broken world cannot express it precisely. We live in a system that doesn't work, which is part of a larger system that does work.

Jesus brings that larger system into our system, the Logos that cannot be expressed but only experienced in the flesh, the eternal moral perfection that cannot be litigated but only lived: the kingdom of heaven.

There is a debate among translators. Does Jesus say, "The kingdom of heaven is within you," or does he say it is "among you" or "in your midst"?[57] The Greek word *entos* seems clearly to mean "within," but the context suggests it could have the other meanings, and there are instances of its being used that way in other texts.

To me, the argument itself is deceiving. We are each simultaneously one and part of the many, individuals mysteriously woven into our culture, our tribe, our alliances, and the human race. If the kingdom of heaven is within you, it is also within the people standing next to you and is therefore among you as well. And since it can be lived out only in freedom and not under constraint, the freedom of the people next to you and your freedom are all of absolute worth, not only to each of you but to everyone else.

We have been given the complex task of making laws that protect us from evil yet somehow maintain the individual's freedom to choose or not to choose the good. We cannot, like Robespierre, terrorize our neighbor into virtue.

In the Romantic era—as gospel faith began to fade—all the answers that had rested on the authority of Jesus began to become questions again. What is truth? Who is there within us—what is our soul? And this question too: How do we solve the paradox of freedom? In this book I have examined the answers of poets because I believe these are poetic questions. The answers ultimately must be experienced, as art is experienced; they can't be explained as theology, philosophy, and law are explained. That is why the law of Moses was not enough. Jesus had to live and die and rise again because life is the ultimate work of art and his life is the ultimate life by which we guide our own.

A rich man—some sort of ruler—came to Jesus and asked, "What must I do to inherit eternal life?"

It's a remarkable moment because the question is so direct. What acts must I perform to enter the kingdom?

This story is told in Matthew, Mark, and Luke—the three synoptic gospels—with only minor variations.[58] Jesus tells the man that he should obey the ten commandments. Don't murder, don't commit adultery, don't steal, don't bear false witness, honor your father and your mother—these are in all three versions of the story. Mark adds don't defraud. Matthew adds love your neighbor as yourself.

What's interesting to me about all these lists is what they leave out: the specifically religious commandments. Have no other gods. Remember the Sabbath. Don't take the Lord's name in vain. Jesus mentions none of these.

When the rich man says he has always followed the commandments, Jesus tells him there is one more thing: he should sell all he has, give the money to the poor, and follow him.

This instruction has forced endless generations of pastors to assure their wealthy parishioners that that's not what he really meant.

But what did he mean?

When Romanticism comes under attack by those who preen themselves on being children of the Enlightenment, a frequent target is the famous French philosopher Jean-Jacques Rousseau. Rousseau does indeed say many false things beautifully—that is how you become a famous French philosopher. If German philosophers have the talent of rendering essential truths wholly incomprehensible, their French counterparts have the opposite gift of saying eloquently what has no bearing on reality at all.

"Man is born free, but he is everywhere in chains," Rousseau wrote.[59] It's a lovely phrase, truly, but absurd. It represents a strain of Romantic thought which can't be laid wholly at the feet of Rousseau but into which he often strayed. The idea is that we are born blank slates—free entities—on which anything at all can be written. Indeed, in our golden days of primitivity, we were "noble savages" until civilization corrupted and enslaved us.[60] We need only rebuild civilization from the ground up and we can write *goodness* and *equality* on our blank slates and thereafter be equal and good.

This is the heart of radicalism. These are the ideas that ultimately infected the French Revolution and transformed it into the Terror. The revolutionaries began to feel that if only they could remove the oppressive and corrupt laws and rites and rituals of civilization, if only they could erase the sinful past and tear down all the statues of famous sinners, if only they could declare a new year with new names for all the months and days and just imagine there's no heaven and no religion too, why then, they would release man's oh-so-wonderful original self into a utopian tomorrow and the world would live as one.

How do you begin? To paraphrase the famous French philosopher Denis Diderot, you must strangle the last king with the entrails of the last priest!

The idea of man as a blank slate corrupted by society and

perfectible by perfect systems always tends toward mass murder and tyranny. Because man is not a blank slate and not perfectible. In order to make society perfect, you really have to kill all the people first.

If instead of being a famous French philosopher, Rousseau had wanted to speak the truth, he might have said something more like this: "We are born naked, but we are everywhere in clothes."

Civilization is a costumed play in which we act out traditions built upon our human nature. That nature is no blank slate at all: it is fleshly, it is gendered, it is full of inequalities and idiot desires that must be curtailed. Society is humanity's attempt to organize what it finds beautiful in itself into a performance of the Logos. There is no wholly logical reason why women should adorn themselves one way and men another, why priests or judges should wear costumes others don't, why we should exchange rings at weddings or splash water on our heads at our conversion. These customs are, at their best, a kind of poetry with which we express the truth and beauty of the human condition that cannot be expressed otherwise.

Like most of us, maybe all of us, I have personally experienced the power of such rites and rituals. I saw no reason to marry my live-in girlfriend. For all intent and purposes, we were already married, I thought. Yet when I did marry her, at the moment the ceremony ended, I knew we had been transformed and she had become my wife forever, flesh of my flesh. Likewise, I submitted to baptism with a shrug. I thought it was a meaningless rite since my heart was already converted. But arising from my knees at the font, I discovered my soul had been suddenly cleansed and enlarged and set free. Ceremony blessed me when blessed reason served me ill.

Shakespeare has the hero-king Henry V deal with this enigma on the eve of his remarkable victory against the French at Agincourt. With his troops weary and sick and vastly outnumbered, the king feels the weight of the world on his shoulders through a sleepless night. He reflects bitterly that the only difference between him and the ordinary man who sleeps at peace is "ceremony." He laments that ceremony gives him no magic kingly abilities but only burdens him with the anxieties of kingship. Yes, he has power over other men, but in the hour of possible disaster, he envies those men because they are free of his crushing responsibilities.

"What art thou, thou idle ceremony?" he asks.

> What kind of god art thou . . .
> Art thou aught else but place, degree and form,
> Creating awe and fear in other men?[61]

And yet, moments later, almost in the same breath, he prays to the "God of battles" for victory. And as he does, he details the rites and rituals he has performed to erase his father's sin of deposing the rightful king, Richard II. He has reburied Richard's body, paid the poor to pray for forgiveness, and endowed chapels where the priests sing for Richard's soul. Ceremony is the natural means of speaking into the supernatural realm of meaning. When we stand before God, the ceremonies become filled with those inexpressible truths they somehow express.

Because Henry is a good man, he lives into the meaning of the ceremony of royalty. He becomes what it demands he become: a great king, those words—*great king*—made flesh.

But, of course, not all men are good, and power can corrupt the best of them. Some—maybe most—get into office and live into nothing but the worst instincts of their own pleasure-seeking egos. And as institutions become sclerotic and corrupt, as oppression and inequality become too offensive to bear, the people who are stuck with the roles of peasants in the play of civilization ask themselves, "Why does the king get a crown and not me? How did he become the star of the show? Isn't it just an arbitrary adornment—place, degree, and form? Might I not wear that power just as well? Might we not each be kings, or all be kings together?"

What every radical knows is that tradition and ceremony can protect the reign of the corrupt and maintain rotten institutions past the point of their usefulness. What every conservative knows is that tradition and ceremony are all that stand between us and barbarism, the rule of pleasure and power. As the conservative sheriff says in Cormac McCarthy's novel *No Country for Old Men*, "Any time you quit hearin Sir and Mam the end is pretty much in sight."[62]

Jesus' response to the rich man—like his response to those who accused the adulteress—is perfectly calibrated to please neither radical nor conservative.

He lists those commandments which are the moral law known to all people in all cultures, what C. S. Lewis called the *Tao*. That's why he leaves out the religious commandments. He is reaching out beyond the chosen people in their time in order to speak to all people at all times.

Don't murder, don't steal. Your neighbor has the right to life, in other words. He has the right to his property. All truly human civilization is based on these two realities.

Don't commit adultery, don't bear false witness, don't defraud. You have the responsibility to be authentic: to speak the truth and to do what you say you'll do. All truly human civilization requires this.

Honor your father and your mother. Acknowledge this simple fact: there is no new wisdom. You are not going to reinvent the moral order. If you think you have, think again. You are not going to change human nature. If you think you will, stop whatever you're doing before someone gets hurt. Your traditions are the road that brought you to your present understanding. If you find the truth and beauty those traditions express, you can take that road into a better future. Destroy the road and there's only a wilderness of blood in every direction.

This is the core of the moral law. It cannot be thrown away. It will not be reasoned away. These are the self-evident truths by which all other truths are proven.

It is only when the rich man says he has fulfilled all the *Tao* commandments that Jesus adds, "Give away everything you own and follow me, the incarnation of the one true God."

Hearing this last commandment, the rich man goes away dispirited. It is difficult for those who have the good things in life to tear their hearts away from them and choose to direct themselves toward something even better.

But with God all things are possible.

It is a paradox within a paradox. You have to be free to choose the *Tao*, or it is not the *Tao*. But only by choosing the *Tao* can you begin to become truly free. "Everyone who commits sin is a slave to sin," says Jesus. I have seen this again and again. I've known one or two murderers, quite a few thieves, too many adulterers, and more liars than honest men. Each in his degree was a slave and miserable. Only the person who chooses virtue and authenticity can be slowly shaped into a soul unchained. He's the one who can let go of what the world calls good and follow Christ into the Logos life, to be the flesh made Word, to live a life like the Scriptures, figurative—a life that expresses the truth underlying the two great commandments that, in turn, underlie all the others: love God and love your neighbor as yourself.

But then, who is your neighbor?

To me, the weirdest parable in the Gospels is the parable of the Good Samaritan. I have never heard anyone preach a sermon on its weirdness, and when I've pointed out its weirdness to pastors and priests, I've received nothing but blank looks in answer. I suppose there is some small possibility that everyone else on earth is right and I am wrong. But I doubt it. I think we just know the story too well to really hear how very strange it is.

Jesus tells a lawyer that he will inherit eternal life if he loves God and loves his neighbor. The lawyer, being a lawyer, asks, "Who is my neighbor?" Jesus answers with the story of a man who gets mugged by robbers and thrown in a ditch. A priest goes by without helping him. A member of the holy tribe of Levi does the same. Finally, a Samaritan comes along. The Jews despised the Samaritans. But it's the Samaritan who gives the injured man help.

Having told this story, Jesus asks the lawyer, "Which of these three, do you think, proved to be a neighbor to the man who fell among the robbers?" Of course, the lawyer answers, "The one who showed him mercy"—the Samaritan. And Jesus says, "Go and do likewise."[63]

Go and do likewise? Think about this. Jesus says, "Love your neighbor." The lawyer asks, "Who is my neighbor?" Which is to say, Whom shall I love? Jesus says, "A man was mugged, a despised Samaritan helped him—who was *his* neighbor?" Clearly, the mugged man stands for the lawyer, and the answer to the lawyer's question "Who is my neighbor?" is "The person who does the right thing, no matter what race he is." The natural and obvious moral of the story is: Judge a man by the content of his character, and if he acts like your neighbor, love him as yourself, even if he is a Samaritan. This seems like a good, moral, logical, and practical piece of advice.

But according to Jesus, the moral is: the Samaritan is your neighbor, so go and do what the Samaritan did.

This is really bizarre and not very logical at all. Love your neighbor. Your neighbor is the person who treats you kindly. Therefore, treat people kindly. By that logic, the Samaritan now has to love the injured traveler as himself because by helping him he became his neighbor. Practically, that makes no sense. The injured man may be a terrible person. Why should the Samaritan love him just because he helped him out of trouble? The traveler should love the Samaritan for giving him help, no? Not the other way around. It is really as if Jesus told a reasonable parable, and some tippler scribe rewrote the moral while drunk off his feet.

But because this illogical advice fits in with everything else Jesus says, I think the weird version is actually the right one.

First, we have to realize what Jesus does not say. He does not say treat people kindly and they will become better people. That might be true on occasion, but it is by no means the rule. Many nasty and wicked people act out of their own desires and beliefs no matter what we do, and will not respond to kindness at all. We did not create them and no action of ours can convert them. It is pure narcissism to suppose we have that power.

In fact, Jesus never says his injunctions will make the world a better place. Give your money to the poor, he says, but the poor you will always have with you. Be the light of the world and the salt of the earth, he says, but the world will hate you. Follow me, and, congratulations, you'll probably get crucified. Your only reward will be in the kingdom of heaven, which is within you.

Jesus says, "Love your enemies and pray for those who persecute you," not because it will transform your enemies into your friends. He says do it "so that you may be sons of your Father who is in heaven. For he makes his sun rise on the evil and on the good, and sends rain on the just and on the unjust."[64] Typical religions call upon us to do good and be good. But Christ calls on us to "be perfect as your heavenly Father is perfect."

That's another line that keeps the pastors busy with explanations. But the Greek word translated as perfect here is τέλειοι: be complete, fulfill your *telos*, your purpose, as God fulfills his. Live completely into what God made you to be. The Greek word for sin, *hamartia*, means to miss that target, to miss your *telos*.

"Unless you change and become like little children, you will never enter the kingdom of heaven."[65] This is not because children are good or pliable or obedient or credulous—have you ever met one? It is because Wordsworth was right: "Heaven lies about us in our infancy!"[66] There is a oneness with the world that little children have, a oneness with their own nature that is gone almost in the first moment of self-consciousness, as Wordsworth also knew. That oneness is the map into the self we were made to become. And all of us have lost our way, except for one, except for Jesus, who did grow into himself, completely, who did not miss the target.

Now Jesus is trying to teach us the trick of it. He wants us to see the world as he sees it, to know it as he knows it, to understand our bodies and ourselves as the language of the Logos, so that his joy may be in us and our joy may be full, so that we may have life in abundance and eternal life in the kingdom of heaven which is within us.

This, for me, is the key that unlocks the Sermon on the Mount.

5. THE SERMON ON THE MOUNT: JESUS AND THE SOUL

Now when Jesus saw the crowds, he went up on a mountainside and sat down. His disciples came to him, and he began to teach them.[67]

In one of his most profound letters, John Keats wrote, "Scenery is fine—but human nature is finer—the sward is richer for the tread of a real nervous English foot—the Eagle's nest is finer for the Mountaineer has looked into it. Are these facts or prejudices?"[68]

Coleridge understood that the interplay between human consciousness and nature was in fact an interplay of nature with itself. Living and dying, we are part of the eternal system of life and death. We are the part that knows itself.

Yet strangely, in the interplay of consciousness with nature, something greater than nature is revealed. Wordsworth felt it in "a sense sublime,"

Of something far more deeply interfused,
Whose dwelling is the light of setting suns,
And the round ocean and the living air,
And the blue sky, and in the mind of man:
A motion and a spirit, that impels
All thinking things, all objects of all thought,
And rolls through all things.[69]

When consciousness knows nature truly, it discovers something beyond nature, something supernatural. Keats recorded this experience in his perfect poem "To Autumn," where the season of life and death became a person

Sitting careless on a granary floor,
Thy hair soft-lifted by the winnowing wind.

This was but a fleeting fragment, a mental souvenir in an increasingly godless age, of what Moses saw when he looked upon the burning bush. He too saw nature's eternal system of life and death become a person. From the fire that never goes out on the bush that is never destroyed, he heard a voice speak its name to him, a mind answering his mind: I AM THAT I AM.

"Are these facts or prejudices?" Keats asked. If a burning bush speaks and there is no one there to hear it, does it still say, "I AM"? Is there really a God, or when nature seems to us the creation of a consciousness like our own, are we simply seeing a reflection of ourselves?

Jesus is the response to those questions, the most rational response, I think. Because we can know the world through numbers—through immaterial ideas that accurately describe material reality—because the statement that life is absurd is absurd, because beauty is truth and truth is beauty, we know our minds are made to find the meaning in creation. Only a human being—his life, his death, his eternal life—can provide us with what Coleridge called the "total idea," the idea of which each of us expresses his small piece, his soul. The life, the miracles, the death, the resurrection of Jesus tell us that the mind isn't spinning mere fictions. Our interaction with the world is fractal work: creation within creation, metaphor within metaphor, trinity within trinity proceeding out of and representing the Trinity that is the source and life of it all.

When we understand our inner experience as a little Genesis, the ongoing creation of creation, we begin to understand that we are fearfully and wonderfully made in the image of God. And when we love God and love his image—our neighbor, enemy, and friend alike—we begin to move close to the Jesus mind, the total idea.

That too, that love, is an image of the Trinity: a three-part relationship between one and another by means of the spirit that connects them. Love is the key to knowing the creation truly because creation is the act of love by a Trinity that is an eternal act of love.

Jesus calls on us to treat the injured stranger as the Samaritan did so we will see the injured stranger as God sees him. He wants us to love our enemies so that we will treat even evil people as God does, shining on them with the same sun as he shines on the good, feeding them as he feeds the birds of the air, adorning them like the lilies of the field. He wants us to do these things not to change the world but to know the world and by knowing the world to change ourselves to be more in accordance with him.

The nature of this change is, I think, what Keats was moving toward when he defined the "poetical character"[70] as the mind that takes as much delight in light as in darkness, that "has no Identity"[71] itself and makes no judgment, but lives with the negative capability of enduring uncertainty and speculation. It simply creates what it creates with "gusto," with joy.

Because our lives are stories—works of art—art is practice for love. It is practice in including other stories, good and evil, within our own story. This is why I think Shakespeare, while not a Christian writer per se, is the most Christian writer. He "has as much delight in conceiving an [evil] Iago as a [lovable] Imogen," as Keats put it.[72] He shines his light on the good and the bad, the just and the unjust alike.

This is also why all good art is worthy, not just the art that says the "right thing," the thing that agrees with my worldview. Any work that puts its characters' minds in mine, any work that puts the artist's mind in mine, any work that gives me the inexpressible heart of its creator enlarges me and teaches me to see the creator of all.

This is why I believe Jesus said, "Judge not lest you be judged." He was not warning us about hypocrisy. He was giving us the first and central rule of seeing the Logos-world he sees. We do not want to follow that rule, none of us does, not for a moment, not at all. We want to keep committing original sin, like the traumatized child keeps reenacting his trauma. We want to seize the knowledge of good and evil for ourselves and pass judgment on the souls of others as if we were God on high. Jesus is pointing the way back to Eden: judge not.

Such acts of love may not change the unlovable. They may not change society even a little. Our enemies may remain our enemies even when we love them—they probably will. And even when we don't pass judgment on it, sin remains sin because the Logos remains the Logos and you can fail to live into your piece of the Logos, your soul. You can miss that target.

There will still be practical matters to take care of. Criminals will still have to be imprisoned to protect society. Enemies will still have to be battled and sometimes killed. A poor man may take your money and spend it on alcohol and drugs and then be poor again. One way or another, the world will continue to be the world, whatever fresh disguise modernity puts on it.

But to love without judgment transforms the lover. To love as God loves, to behave toward the world as God does, to shine on the good and evil alike gives us eyes to see with, ears to hear. You begin to lose your life—your opinions, your fake and precious virtue—your identity, as Keats said—and so you find your life, your true life, the perfected identity God made in you from the start. You become like a little child again. You recapture the idea of yourself that lived in God's mind even before he formed you in the womb. You grow toward the idea of yourself that will live on in his mind eternally.

Judge not—a simple command, but not an easy one.

I could not understand the Sermon on the Mount—it seemed to me like a series of dubious assertions and impossible commands—because I was trying to understand a philosophy instead of trying to get to know a man, instead of trying to see what he saw, and experience the world as he did.

Jesus is not an idol. He is not a moveless statue of a god. He is fully a man who fully embodied God. He lived once in time as we do now. He grew and developed and came into himself as every man must. But he was perfect as his Father in heaven was perfect. He was sinless: he did not miss the target. He came into himself completely.

It is not that Christ is who we should be. It is that he became what we are trying to become.

The Sermon on the Mount is a map of that experience, a way to recreate that experience in our own minds.

Blessed are the poor in spirit, for theirs is the kingdom of heaven.[73]

Everyone who has ever had a spiritual revelation says the same thing. Everyone who has had a moment of high clarity in which he suddenly sees the underlying reality of the world as it truly is says this: "For one second, I understood that everything was all right, all of it."

"All will be well," as the mystic Julian of Norwich put it, "and all manner of thing shall be well."[74]

This is what the Beatitudes tell us. The mourning will be comforted. The meek will inherit the earth. The persecuted will enter the kingdom. This is the greater system within which our broken system lives. This is the world we are looking at, the real world, the whole world. This is what we have to learn to see every day.

Everything is actually all right. All will be well.

You have heard that it was said to the people long ago, "You shall not murder, and anyone who murders will be subject to judgment." But I tell you that anyone who is angry with a brother or sister will be subject to judgment . . . You have heard that it was said, "You shall not commit adultery." But I tell you that anyone who looks at a woman lustfully has already committed adultery with her in his heart.[75]

It is easy to hear these words as a judgment. Don't lust. Don't be angry. It's a sin. Like adultery. Like murder.

But Jesus did not come to judge the world. He came to save

the world. He said so. This is simply a description: lust and adultery are things that the body does. Anger and murder are things that the body does. Each flows into the other, one thing, flesh into flesh.

The Logos-self doesn't live according to the flesh but according to the spirit, not according to the body but, through the body, according to the meaning the body is meant to express, the soul. That soul can only be located in love because it is the creation of the Logos, which is love.

You can learn to experience this through practice and discipline. The flesh does not discriminate between experiences, but you can. When I played tennis, losing felt like dying to me. I wanted victory so badly, I was sometimes tempted to cheat to get it. I had to force myself not to. Every player knows this feeling. And yet, I was a third-rate club player. I had no money on the line, no reputation, no meaningful career advancement. But my body couldn't tell the difference. It reacted to a situation with no real-world stakes as if it were do or die.

Much the same thing happens when you desire a sexual partner without love or grow enraged with a friend over a hurtful remark. Your body reacts to an essentially meaningless interchange as if life itself were at stake. You are, as Jesus says, committing the act of adultery or murder in your heart because your life has become separated from the true meaning of life, your flesh is disconnected from the spirit it was made to express. This is a pretty good definition of being in a state of sin.

In relationships, as in sports, you have to realign your body with the reality of its true meaning. An athlete can make every effort to win and yet play fairly if he aligns himself with the fact that excellence of both performance and character are the true meaning of every game. If you can't play without cheating, don't play. Likewise, if the eye of lust causes you to offend against the meaning of sex, pluck it out, so to speak. If your hand is raised in anger, cut it off, so to speak. Learn to experience lust and rage—fear and anxiety and envy—as a shot wide of the mark of true meaning—*hamartia*. Aim the flesh toward its *telos*: be perfect.

The method by which you do that is love, a love like God's that shines on the just and the unjust. The more you experience that love, the more it shapes you, the more the language of your body comes to speak it, the more your body speaks the soul, who you are. It is not a matter of pretending. You don't have to pretend your body doesn't feel lust or anger or anxiety or envy—of course it does. Of course it will. But by a practice of perception, honed by action, you can learn to see that the Logos-self is the real self. Fidelity. Charity. Forgiveness. These are disciplines that train you to know true meaning.

You already know you are not your flesh alone, not your flesh without its spiritual meaning. You have experienced the satisfactions of lust or rage, adultery or violence, lying and playing it safe. They are very fine satisfactions: pleasure, vengeance, profit, and security. Goods of the flesh which the flesh earned.

But you also know the shame you hide from yourself, the self-disdain you project onto those around you, the smallness you don't even dare to acknowledge, the desperate and increasing need to condemn others in order to perform a virtue you know you don't have, the need to tell lies and then more lies to yourself and all the world.

That—that soul in sin-forged manacles—is you. It is, at least, the ruin of the person God made you to be: the shriveled shadow held within its cell, striving to break free into the shape of its bright entirety.

The way to that freedom is just outside the prison door.
Behold, he stands at the door and knocks.

A good tree cannot bear bad fruit, and a bad tree cannot bear
good fruit. Every tree that does not bear good fruit is cut down
and thrown into the fire.[76]

I hear people say that Christianity is cheap virtue because it
threatens you with hell if you are bad and promises heaven if you
are good. The people who say this are no doubt good because of the
sheer angelic sweetness of their natures. Or something.

But it is not a threat to say: If you don't exercise, you will be
flabby. If you don't read, you will be ignorant. This is just the way
things are.

If your life expresses your soul, the idea of you in the mind of
God, then that is how you will live in the mind of God forever. If
your life expresses another idea that lives elsewhere, you will live
elsewhere. Forever.

The Sermon on the Mount is not a philosophy. It is Jesus telling
you what he sees: the way things truly are.

Therefore everyone who hears these words of mine and puts
them into practice is like a wise man who built his house on
the rock.[77]

When you see the world as it truly is, you begin to break out of
the flow of its glorious illusions. You need not worry for tomorrow.
You need not bother to make a show of your righteousness. You
need not pray in endless displays of virtue. You need not devote
your life to storing up treasure of any kind.

We are busy with many things, but only one thing is necessary: See, if you have eyes to see with. Hear, if you have ears to hear.

6. The End: Jesus and Eternity

The Son of Man must suffer many things and be rejected by the elders, the chief priests and the teachers of the law, and he must be killed and on the third day be raised to life.[78]

Everything that Jesus did was both wholly itself and wholly a metaphor for its meaning. This was true of nothing so much as his death.

Theologians—pastors—Christians—discuss what it meant. A sacrifice for the sins of mankind. A payment for the transgression in Eden. All the Old Testament drawn into his person so that he became the sacrificial paschal lamb and the angel of death passed over us and we were set free.

But it was fully death too, wholly death, his death. Which points to something else I think Jesus had to experience in order to be who he was and to know who we are.

The gap between matter and meaning, between flesh and spirit, between Logos and the world, is the place where tragedy lives and where we live.

Cradle to grave, the Logos life is a tragic life.

When my wife and I visited Israel a few years back, we toured all the religious sites. We walked the road Jesus is supposed to have taken to the cross. We saw the place where he is supposed to have been crucified. We entered the tomb where he is said to have been laid.

I was largely immune to the sentimental impact of these places. Maybe I didn't really believe they were authentic. Or maybe the garish shrines built around them or the crowds of tourists put me off. In any case, I was more impressed by a worn slab of stone in the entryway of the original temple because Jesus might have actually stepped on it. I was more deeply moved by the scenery around the Sea of Galilee because that was the scenery he saw.

But above the city of Jerusalem, on the Mount of Olives, near the garden of Gethsemane, there is a place called the Church of the Agony built on the spot where Jesus is supposed to have gone after the Last Supper. Inside the church, there's an exposed slab of bedrock which is where Jesus is supposed to have fallen when he prayed. Like most of these sites, this one is disputed. It seems too close to the road for Jesus to have gone there for privacy.

But there, I had what was only the second mystical experience of my life.

I walked into the church without expectations—dubious about the location, weary of tourist attractions. I wandered around inside, distracted. Then I came within sight of the rock.

Suddenly, a deep darkness of anguish filled me. It was not my anguish. I did not feel anguished myself. Instead, I felt inhabited by an inescapable torment of fear and sorrow that was not mine. I have never had any other experience like it. Someone else's emotions had sprung to life within me.

I remember being startled out of my ennui. My back straightened. I thought, "Oh God, this is really the place!"

Nothing I did changed the feeling inside me. It remained with me when my wife and I left the church. We came upon a choir singing. We stood and listened.

After about half an hour, the anguish faded away.

There is a Zen story about a master named Yantou. Bandits raided his monastery and murdered him. The people said they could hear his dying scream for ten miles around. He was so enlightened, so awake to life, that he suffered at a more intense level than the rest of us.

Jesus died a bad death, beaten, tortured, slowly killed. But there have been worse deaths. There can always be worse. What made this death the worst of all was that it was his—the death of the Word made flesh—and he experienced it at the highest intensity possible.

Waiting for his arrest in the garden, he fell on the ground in terror. He sweat blood. He was in an agony of fear and sorrow. He prayed he would not have to drink from the cup of his own martyrdom.

But he was sent not just to live but to perform life. And life is a tragedy.

We don't understand that word very well anymore, the word *tragedy*. Especially in America, where no one ever explained to us it was the central rule of physical existence. In America, as William Dean Howells is supposed to have said, what the public wants is a tragedy with a happy ending. We want to believe that a bad outcome can always be avoided, and when it can't be avoided, we tell ourselves it could have been if only we had gone another way.

That's not how things work. Tragedy is an inevitable conflict of imperatives. It is what happens when a person does what he must do, right or wrong, and, right or wrong, must suffer for what he does. Once the machinery is set in motion, there is no stopping it.

To live is to die. To love is to grieve. To think is to suffer. To speak the truth is to set yourself at daggers drawn with the world.

Jesus was the truth and had to speak the truth, and the world was the world and had to kill him for it: that's tragedy. He wasn't betrayed by an act of evil. He wasn't murdered by a villain. He would not have avoided dying had he been born among another people or in another time. He was the living truth. The religious had to kill him because they were religious. The leaders had to kill him because they were the leaders. The people had to kill him because they were the people. The law had to kill him because it was the law.

That was what it was like to be the truth in the world. That was the tragic nature of the experience. It still is. It would happen all the same this very day.

More than likely, you and I would be in the crowd, screaming, "Give us Barabbas!"

At the Last Supper, he told his disciples, "If you belonged to the world, it would love you as its own. As it is, you do not belong to the world, but I have chosen you out of the world. That is why the world hates you."[79]

Then he went out into the garden.

In the end, when he was hanging nailed to the cross, he cried out, "My God, my God, why have you forsaken me?"[80] It was—like everything he did—both entirely itself and entirely a sign. In this case, it was both a statement of complete despair and a declaration that his despairing death placed him within the psalm that described it—Psalm 22, which begins with the words he cried.

The psalm foretold what would happen to him. "I am . . . scorned by mankind and despised by the people . . . I am poured out like water . . . my heart . . . is melted within my breast . . . they have pierced my hands and feet . . . they stare and gloat over me . . . they divide my garments among them, and for my clothing they cast lots."[81]

But it also tells of God's saving grace and how future generations "will proclaim his righteousness, declaring to a people yet unborn: He has done it!"[82]

His despairing death confirmed he was the fulfillment of the hope of Scripture.

But who would live the Logos life if this were all there was?

Jesus said, "Take up [your] cross and follow me."[83] But who would do it? Why would you? If this tragic world is all there is, why would anyone? A life of truth and beauty, radical love and radical honesty, is a life of joy, but it's also a life at odds with the way of the world. At some point, it will put you in opposition to governments, churches, radicals, conservatives, and the ever-self-righteous mob. Whoever sits on the throne of the day will come to despise you.

You may get lucky. It may happen that your particular nature and its fulfillment in your particular slice of history won't lead you to the hemlock or the cross, the scourge or the fire, the show trial or the public shaming or the unemployment line.

But become as a little child again, become perfect as your Father in heaven is perfect, love your enemy, judge not, live in truth, and some sacrifice—some loss of achievement or pleasure, friendship, community, fame, wealth, or glory—is sure to come. Why do it, unless you are betting that the joy of your wholeness and authenticity is the expression of a greater joy that lies beyond mere life and time, a joy eternal in the presence of a beauty divine?

If you do not believe that life is more than life, it would be madness to do anything but seize the day and live from pleasure to treasure. Better to kowtow to the money men and make your pile. Better to kill an inconvenient unborn child and live unfettered. Better to silence your opponents and seize their fortune than to live in mutual freedom. Better to ditch your promises to your spouse and have a sweet new affair. Better to trade your integrity for success and its trappings. Better to keep your head down and your mouth shut in times of danger.

To choose instead the tragedy of love is to proclaim with your whole life that this kingdom of heaven within you is a kingdom that never ends. When your cross looms in front of you, it won't be enough to "act as if there were a God." You will have to believe, or you will crater.

You don't have to know when history will finish, you don't have to know who is saved and who is damned, you don't have to know the number of the psalms or the names of the apostles or the rulebook that governs the counsel of heaven. But you do have to know what the Logos looks like when it lives on earth and you have to have faith that it lives on forever even after it has been put to death.

The resurrection was like everything else Jesus did: itself and its meaning. He really rose from the dead, and, rising, he showed that the Word speaks the body into existence and that if the body speaks the Word, it becomes part of its endless creation and will be spoken into life without end.

The resurrection tells us that when the flesh becomes the Word, the Word will become flesh again, in a new body, incorruptible. The resurrection says to us: heaven and earth shall pass away but the Word will never pass away.

Therefore, become the Word.

THE ROAD TO EMMAUS

Everything Becomes Literature

Who is the third who walks always beside you?
When I count, there are only you and I together
But when I look ahead up the white road
There is always another one walking beside you
     —T. S. ELIOT, *THE WASTE LAND*

Now that same day [of the resurrection] two of [Jesus' followers] were going to a village called Emmaus, about seven miles from Jerusalem. They were talking with each other about everything that had happened. As they talked and discussed these things with each other, Jesus himself came up and walked along with them; but they were kept from recognizing him.

He asked them, "What are you discussing together as you walk along?"

They stood still, their faces downcast. One of them, named

Cleopas, asked him, "Are you the only one visiting Jerusalem who does not know the things that have happened there in these days?"

"What things?" he asked.

"About Jesus of Nazareth," they replied. "He was a prophet, powerful in word and deed before God and all the people. The chief priests and our rulers handed him over to be sentenced to death, and they crucified him; but we had hoped that he was the one who was going to redeem Israel. And what is more, it is the third day since all this took place. In addition, some of our women amazed us. They went to the tomb early this morning but didn't find his body. They came and told us that they had seen a vision of angels, who said he was alive. Then some of our companions went to the tomb and found it just as the women had said, but they did not see Jesus."

He said to them, "How foolish you are, and how slow to believe all that the prophets have spoken! Did not the Messiah have to suffer these things and then enter his glory?" And beginning with Moses and all the Prophets, he explained to them what was said in all the Scriptures concerning himself.

As they approached the village to which they were going, Jesus continued on as if he were going farther. But they urged him strongly, "Stay with us, for it is nearly evening; the day is almost over." So he went in to stay with them.

When he was at the table with them, he took bread, gave thanks, broke it and began to give it to them. Then their eyes were opened and they recognized him, and he disappeared from their sight. They asked each other, "Were not our hearts burning within us while he talked with us on the road and opened the Scriptures to us?"

They got up and returned at once to Jerusalem.[1]

In the end, everything becomes literature. Whatever is not forgotten must be told. Whatever is told unfolds itself in time. Whatever unfolds in time becomes a story.

Stories express a meaning. If this were not so, we would not tell them. Lazarus was raised from the dead, but where is he now? Dead again. So who is Lazarus to us? The only reason to tell his story is because of what his story means.

But which meaning is the real meaning? The truth, after all, is a kind of silence. Things just are. Life just happens. Stories—even our life stories—are simply chains of events. When we interpret their meanings, are we connecting the natural sphere to a supernatural sphere of moral reality, or are we molding meaningless silence into a narrative that expresses the prejudices of our humanity in its particular culture at its particular time?

The materialists tell us that our narratives are fictions. We made them and they can be remade in any way we like so that they will be better, more true, more just. To me, their position is irrational, self-contradictory. The very idea that there is some better, more true, more just story tells us there is a sphere above nature in which the immaterial concepts *good*, *truth*, and *justice* exist. It is this sphere true stories describe, and our stories will not be true if they do not describe it.

Stories have a purpose then. They are a language for communicating a type of reality that can be communicated in no other way: that interplay of human consciousness with reality in which we experience the good, the true, and the beautiful.

We may be deluded in that experience. We may see water on a bone-dry highway or mistake infatuation for love or convince ourselves that slavery is justifiable. But the fact that we may be mistaken tells us that we are capable of getting it right. It matters how we mold the silent truth. It matters what stories we tell.

In the end, life becomes literature, and literature has meaning because life has meaning.

When the risen Christ met his disciples on the road to Emmaus, his sole work was the work of interpreting literature, helping them to understand what their literature meant. He gave them a new way of reading their holy scriptures and that reading changed not just their lives but the entire human world. From that time on, to those who believe, the stories of Jewish history became not just themselves but also types and portents foreshadowing the coming of Christ. When Jonah spent three days in the belly of the whale, he symbolized Jesus' spending three days in the belly of death. The twelve tribes of Israel predicted the twelve apostles. The sacrificed Passover lamb was the harbinger of Jesus, the sacrificed lamb of God.

Prophecies now came clear. The mysterious visions of Isaiah were revealed to predict the coming of Jesus seven hundred years in advance: unto us a child is born, a son is given, the Prince of Peace, pierced for our transgressions. The Jewish law became symbolic. You don't have to be circumcised in the flesh anymore, because in Christ "you were also circumcised with a circumcision not performed by human hands."[2] Such rules were "a shadow of the things that were to come; the reality, however, is found in Christ."[3]

Jesus' story—his life, his words, his works, his death, his resurrection—was the meaning of their stories. It had been all along.

Through this interpretation, the Bible became universal. Its stories became all our stories. Its central commandments became the world's. The promise of salvation was no longer a tribal promise but a promise to each individual which united all individuals in a single new race, the body of Christ.

Jesus' story was now the meaning of each of our stories and all of them together.

If what he said was true, then no honest heart can deny him. Even in an age of unbelief, every man and woman who sets out on the road to truth will find themselves on the road to Emmaus, an invisible third walking beside them. All nature will speak his presence to them. Even the bread they eat and the wine they drink will become his flesh and his blood. Every song and every new creation will speak the Word that was spoken at the beginning. And even this road, this hard road we're on, will not take us away from Jerusalem in the end but to a new Jerusalem, redeemed.

The world has told us that all our truths are merely stories, but this man who walks with us on the road to Emmaus, he told us that all our stories are really truths—truths in human form, which is the form of beauty, which is the form divine, which is his form, the form of the Word made flesh.

And while he was speaking, did we not feel our hearts burning within us?

NOTES

INTRODUCTION

1. Editors of Encyclopaedia Britannica, "Nicene Creed," *Britannica*, https://www.britannica.com/topic/Nicene-Creed, accessed May 15, 2020.

2. Timothy Keller, *Shaped by the Gospel: Doing Balanced, Gospel-Centered Ministry in Your City* (Grand Rapids: Zondervan, 2016), 27.

3. There's a delightful little nineteenth-century horror novel on this subject: *The Private Memoirs and Confessions of a Justified Sinner* by James Hogg. In it, a man becomes convinced that he is predestined for salvation by faith alone and so his actions don't matter. You can guess the results, but they're still deliciously evil.

4. John 15:15.

5. William Wordsworth, *The Prelude* (London: Penguin, 1995), lines 692–93.

6. Joseph Heller, *Catch-22* (New York: Simon and Schuster, 1961), 180.

7. Jacques Barzun, *Classic, Romantic, and Modern*, 2nd ed. (Chicago: Univ. of Chicago Press, 1961), xv–xvii.

8. M. H. Abrams, *Natural Supernaturalism: Tradition and Revolution in Romantic Literature* (New York: Norton, 1971), 13.

9. C. S. Lewis, "Christianity and Culture," *Theology* 40, no. 237 (March 1940): 176.

10. David Fuller, ed., *William Blake: Selected Poetry and Prose* (Harlow, UK: Pearson Education, 2000), 360.

CHAPTER 1: THE IMMORTAL EVENING

1. Lynne Truss, "A Genius for Failure: The Life of Benjamin Robert Haydon by Paul O'Keeffe," *Sunday Times*, August 9, 2009.

2. Colin Martin, "Anatomical Art," *The Lancet* no. 370 (2007): 558.

3. Benjamin Robert Haydon, *The Life, Letters and Table Talk of Benjamin Robert Haydon* (New York: Scribner, Armstrong, and Co., 1876), 63.

4. Suzie Grogan, *John Keats: Poetry, Life and Landscapes* (Barnsley, UK: Pen and Sword Books, 2021).

5. John Keats, "Addressed to the Same," in *John Keats' Poetry Manuscripts at Harvard*, ed. Jack Stillinger (Cambridge, MA: Belknap Press, 1990), 20.

6. John Keats, *Letters of John Keats to His Family and Friends*, ed. John Barnard (London: MacMillan, 1925), 2.

7. Benjamin Robert Haydon, "B.R. Haydon on Some Contemporaries: A New Letter," letter to Mary Russell Mitford (February 12, 1824), *The Review of English Studies* 26, no. 102 (1975): 189.

8. T. S. Eliot, *Shakespeare and the Stoicism of Seneca* (London: Folcroft Library Editions, 1973).

9. Jacques Barzun, *Classic, Romantic, and Modern* (Boston: Little, Brown, 1961), 42.

10. Samuel T. Coleridge, letter to John Thelwall, *Letters of Samuel Coleridge* (New York: Houghton Mifflin and Co., 1895), 164.

11. Clarke Olney, *Benjamin Robert Haydon: Historical Painter* (Atlanta: Univ. of Georgia Press, 1952), 131.

12. John Keats, *The Poetical Works of John Keats* (London: Macmillan, 1884).

13. Olney, *Benjamin Robert Haydon*, 131.

14. Ibid.

15. Edward Verrall Lucas, *The Life of Charles Lamb* (London: G. P. Putnam's Sons, 1905), xvii.

16. Denise Gigante, *The Great Age of the English Essay* (New Haven: Yale Univ. Press, 2008), 336.

17. Sarah Burton, *A Double Life: A Biography of Charles and Mary Lamb* (Eastbourne, UK: Gardners Books, 2003).
18. Olney, *Benjamin Robert Haydon*, 132.
19. Stanley Plumly, *The Immortal Evening: A Legendary Dinner with Keats, Wordsworth, and Lamb* (New York: Norton, 2014), 180.
20. Olney, *Benjamin Robert Haydon*, 132.
21. Ibid., 133.
22. Ibid., 134.

CHAPTER 2: WHO'S THERE?

1. Benjamin Haydon, *Life of Benjamin Robert Haydon: His Autobiography and Journals* (London: Longman, Brown, Green, and Longmans, 1853), 388.
2. Benjamin Robert Haydon, *Neglected Genius: The Diaries of Benjamin Robert Haydon, 1808–1846* (London: Hutchinson, 1990).
3. Benjamin Robert Haydon, *The Life, Letters and Table Talk of Benjamin Robert Haydon* (New York: Scribner, Armstrong, and Co., 1876), 304.
4. William Blake, "The Mental Traveller," in *The Poetical Works of William Blake*, ed. John Sampson (London: Oxford Univ. Press, 1908), line 62.
5. Matthew Arnold, "Dover Beach," in *English Poetry III: From Tennyson to Whitman* (New York: P. F. Collier & Son, 1909–14), lines 21–28.
6. Larry Siedentop, *Inventing the Individual: The Origins of Western Liberalism* (Cambridge, MA: Belknap Press, 2017).
7. Seamus Heaney, "Song," from *Field Work* (New York: Farrar, Straus, and Giroux, 1979).
8. Much of the following is my reaction to Stephen Greenblatt's wonderful *Hamlet in Purgatory* (Princeton: Princeton Univ. Press, 2002).
9. 1 Sam. 28:7–17.
10. Charles Dickens, *A Christmas Carol* (London: Chapman and Hall, 1847), 24.

11. Church of England, *The Book of Common Prayer* (Cambridge, NY: Cambridge Univ. Press, 1662).

12. Stephen Greenblatt, *Hamlet in Purgatory* (Princeton: Princeton Univ. Press, 2001), 240.

13. William Shakespeare, *The Tragedy of Hamlet* (London: Methuen and Co., 1899), 43.

14. Ibid., 18.

15. Ibid., 217.

16. Ibid., 228.

17. Ibid., 3.

CHAPTER 3: UNHALLOWED ARTS

1. Clarke Olney, *Benjamin Robert Haydon: Historical Painter* (Atlanta: Univ. of Georgia Press, 1952), 132.

2. Richard Holmes, *The Age of Wonder: How the Romantic Generation Discovered the Beauty and Terror of Science* (New York: Pantheon, 2008), 318.

3. Wordsworth, *The Prelude*, lines 61–63.

4. John Keats, "On First Looking into Chapman's Homer," in *Poetical Works* (London: Macmillan, 1884), lines 9–14.

5. William Wordsworth, "Nature's Influence, 'My Heart Leaps Up,'" in *The World's Best Poetry*, ed. Bliss Carman, et al. (Philadelphia: John D. Morris and Co., 1904), lines 1–6.

6. Holmes, *Age of Wonder*, 319.

7. William Wordsworth, "Nature's Influence, The Tables Turned," in *World's Best Poetry*, ed. Carman, lines 26–28.

8. John Beer, *William Blake: A Literary Life* (Houndmills, UK: Palgrave Macmillan, 2005), 126.

9. This is the subject of Shakespeare's *A Midsummer Night's Dream*, in which characters are made to feel love through chemical means.

10. Bessel van der Kolk, *The Body Keeps the Score: Brain, Mind, and Body in the Healing of Trauma* (New York: Penguin, 2015), 37.